T0273914

A GARDENER'S GUIDE TO

SUSTAINABLE GARDENING

A GARDENER'S GUIDE TO
SUSTAINABLE GARDENING

The new way to garden

DOUG STEWART

THE CROWOOD PRESS

First published in 2023 by
The Crowood Press Ltd
Ramsbury, Marlborough
Wiltshire SN8 2HR

enquiries@crowood.com

www.crowood.com

© Doug Stewart 2023

All rights reserved. No part of this publication may be reproduced or transmitted in any form or by any means, electronic or mechanical, including photocopy, recording, or any information storage and retrieval system, without permission in writing from the publishers.

British Library Cataloguing-in-Publication Data
A catalogue record for this book is available from the British Library.

ISBN 978 0 7198 4255 9

Dedication

This book is dedicated to those who bring plants to people, and who create community gardens. Together these people create places of social inclusion, personal growth, healing, peace, and ecological regeneration.

They are the best of us.

Image credits

Claudia West/Phyto Studio, p.29, p.30 (top and bottom); Justine Dixon, p.97 (bottom), p.129; Peter Korn, p.58 (top and bottom); Sue Moss, p.101 (bottom three)

Typeset by Simon and Sons
Cover design by Blue Sunflower Creative
Printed and bound in India by Thomson Press Limited

CONTENTS

FOREWORD

Thank you for picking up this book.

The simple fact that you have done so means that you care, and that you are on the cusp of making truly transformative changes to the way you garden. These may be grand-scale structural and functional changes, or they may be small, cumulative interventions, which all have a part to play in protecting our planet and the people within it.

We are all aware that changing the way we live in the world is imperative for the safeguarding of its future. This is as true for what we do in our gardens as it is for how we manage our homes and our travel — but that does not mean it is easy. Revaluating the way we approach the development and cultivation of our garden spaces is complex, for domestic gardeners and professionals alike. Our plants, patios, pots and pergolas are established and maintained with many competing considerations and impacts — both short and long term, local and far afield. For example, where did the patio slabs come from? Have they travelled far? Who quarried the stone and were they paid a fair wage? How long will it last, and will you need to use chemicals to maintain it?

The movement towards a more sustainable way to garden is travelling faster than ever and shows no sign of slowing its pace. While there are some 'no-brainers', like not using peat in growing media and using less plastic, some solutions may be less obvious, more challenging or represent a significant departure from traditional gardening practices. And so they should, if we are to make a true difference.

What is needed is a clear and considered road map to guide the gardener who wants to make a change, and so this book is both welcome and timely. It encourages the gardener to think — to revaluate their spaces and their approach to them, to consider design, build and maintenance practices, and it provides practical solutions for each. I know it is going to be an inspiration and guide for me as I plan my new garden space, and I hope it is for you too.

Dr Suzanne Moss
Head of Education and Learning,
Royal Horticultural Society

CHAPTER 1

UNDERSTANDING SUSTAINABILITY

We cannot solve our problems with the same thinking we used when we created them.

Albert Einstein

Why Write a Book on Sustainable Gardening?

Is the very act of gardening itself not sustainable? After all, gardens are spaces where people connect with nature, they are filled with trees and shrubs, and nature abounds. Green waste is even recycled in composting areas. If, however, we peel back the veneer and take a closer look at the way gardens are managed, many of the activities are far from green. There are often monocultures of grass; maintenance uses fossil fuels and water. Gravels and other materials used in hard landscaping are mined or quarried. Some are even transported from the other side of the world. The movement of plants creates biosecurity risks. The care of gardens often involves pesticides and herbicides. These practices are far from sustainable. To delve a little deeper, we could consider just one element of a garden. For example, we could consider the humble garden bench. What stories could it tell, if only it could speak? Would it tell tales of being carefully fashioned from wood produced in a carefully managed plantation? Of

skilled, well-paid artisan-joiners carefully measuring, cutting and creating? Would it proudly tell of how its sale creates wealth that is shared throughout the supply chain? Of families fed, communities brought together around schools and hospitals?

Or would that bench, if it could speak to the garden visitor, tell a very different story? Would it speak of illegal logging, of being fashioned by children in a dangerous factory, where life-changing injury and death is just around the corner, where the children were sold into bonded labour? Would it speak of the devastation that the illegal felling of timber has on habitat and biodiversity?

If your bench could tell its story, what tales would it tell?

It is easy to forget that buying decisions can have profound effects throughout the supply chain. If strategies were developed to ensure that all purchases were checked off against a list of criteria to ensure principles of fairness, of prosperity for all those in the supply chain and of minimal environmental impact, then it could be argued that our gardens tell stories that we would be proud to be associated with.

The sustainable garden is filled with positive stories: of trees providing ecosystem services to people and to nature; for example, the wide number of invertebrate species supported, the provision of food for caterpillars and nectar for pollinators, or gardens that reduce the risks of flooding and that are filled with birdsong. Special places where people come and experience wellness and improved mental health.

Creating such spaces requires agility of thought. Those who manage gardens and design landscapes make a thousand decisions a day. Each one of these needs rethinking, from the application of spring feeds to the irrigation of garden areas.

Every single maintenance principle needs to be re-evaluated:

- Is it necessary?
- Does it enhance biodiversity?
- Is it regenerative?

Every single input needs to be re-evaluated:

- Is it necessary?
- What is its environmental impact?
- How does it impact on the lives of those in the supply chain?

This process will uncover inconvenient truths. Conventional thinking will be challenged. Scientific principles will be applied. Best practice will be developed.

This book is not intended to be the new rule book, for there are few universal rules that hold true in all gardens and in all situations. Rather this book has been written to be a map, to guide and to be a critical friend to challenge.

Key garden-management principles will be considered. Concepts of ecological garden-management principles will be discussed, along with triggers for both minor and major interventions. These will include operational decisions, for example the management of specific plant health risks. Or strategic decisions, such as the replacement of clusters of pots and containers to reduce the garden's water footprint, or the strategic movement away from short-term plantings to reduce the plastic, peat, water and carbon footprint of the garden.

Containers have high environmental footprints, requiring manufacture, transport, growing media, feed and water.

Plantings of perennials grown in border soil can be used to reduce water and growing media usage.

Rethinking points of intervention is a critical skill for the sustainable gardener. Every action, every mainte-nance decision, has an impact that is far wider and more profound than might at first be thought. The removal of a weed may deny a pollinator a vital food source. The removal of a dead tree may deny habitat to bats and wild birds. This cause and effect was recog-nised by John Muir, the father of modern conservation, who stated: 'When we try to pick out anything by itself, we find it hitched to everything else in the universe.'

What is Sustainability?

It is always useful to define terms. Sustainability is no exception. Sadly, the term sustainable is often over-used as a marketing term. 'Sustainable' is often added as if it is a seasoning before almost any product. Marketeers tempt consumers with 'new sustainable

Aphids are an important part of the garden food web. Lacewings, ladybirds, rove beetles, predatory midges, parasitoid wasps and wild birds use aphids as a food source. When we remove aphids, we find them connected to everything else in the universe, to paraphrase John Muir.

tumble driers' or our 'sustainable burgers'. The question remains: what is it about these products that makes them sustainable? The roots of sustainability lie in social justice, conservation and internationalism. In 1983 the United Nations invited the former Norwegian Prime Minister, Gro Harlem Brundtland, to run the New World Commission on Environment and Development. One of the key findings was that economic development at the cost of ecological health and social equity did not lead to long-lasting prosperity. When the New World Commission on Environment and Development finally reported its findings, it defined sustainable development as:

Development that meets the needs of the present without compromising the ability of future generations to meet their own needs.

This concept can be restated to apply directly to the field of garden management:

To manage gardens and designed landscapes to fully meet our current needs, without compromising the ability of future generations to have the climate, the resources and the freedom to create and manage gardens that will fully meet their needs.

The application of the principles outlined in this statement requires the garden managers of today to carefully consider the potential impact of management decisions. Many gardens pump water from deep boreholes to satisfy their irrigation needs. The water extracted is referred to by water scientists as fossil water. Its use today may deny future generations of a water source. The nitrogen fertilizer used to green up lawn turf is the result of a chemical process, the Haber-Bosch Process, which turns gaseous nitrogen into nitrate, a form a nitrogen that can be taken up by plant roots. This single process releases 1.4 per cent of global carbon emissions. Neither of these activities can be regarded as being sustainable, and so it is necessary to rethink their use. Reducing the water footprint of a garden, or the elimination of synthetic fertilizers, has profound impacts on the management of gardens. Alternative approaches need to be identified and evaluated, and the least worst option selected.

Sustainability has been further defined to include a series of pillars that uphold the core principles stated above.

Sustainability: People, Plants, Planet

The social pillar holds up or promotes concepts of fairness and respect. This includes concepts such as gender equality, gender pay gaps, human rights, the prevention of human slavery, along with striving to reduce social inequalities. This includes combating discrimination and promoting social inclusion. A further aspect of this pillar is the promotion of well-being.

The second pillar is the economic pillar, which is defined as the promotion of responsible sourcing of product, recycling of product and the sourcing of renewable raw materials. It includes the concept of fair pay and the use of renewable energy sources.

The third pillar is environmental. The key principles here are that natural habitats should be preserved, carbon and water footprint reduced, and waste properly managed.

With regard to the first pillar, the role that gardens have in promoting wellness is now widely documented. Mind, the UK mental health charity, published research claiming that over 7 million people report their mental health as benefiting from taking up gardening for the first time during the Covid-19 lockdowns. For many people, gardens became sanctuaries; the very act of gardening became important in the relief of stress and the promotion of mental health. The significant impacts of green spaces on human health have been widely documented in many studies. A consistent finding is that people benefit from being in the presence of plants. These benefits manifest as reduced stress levels, and improved mental health and well-being. Other studies have shown that increasing green infrastructure reduces anti-social behaviour. New initiatives such as green prescribing are being implemented in the UK, where, for example, those who might benefit are prescribed green therapies and are often placed within community horticultural projects as part of their recovery pathway. Gardening and nature therapy generally, are now being referred to as the Natural Health Service.

The significance of the economic pillar becomes apparent when the size and the scope of the gardening industry are considered. The RHS reports on its website that ornamental horticulture could be set to contribute £42 billion to the UK economy and create 760,000 jobs by 2030. By comparison the aerospace industry contributes £35 billion to the UK economy, according to the Office for National Statistics. Horticulture is a major UK industry. The economic pillar requires that supply chains be managed along sustainable lines, and that all those employed in the production of plants and associated products should be valued and fairly rewarded.

The environmental pillar is perhaps the one that gardeners are most familiar with, but it is equally challenging. It introduces the concepts that gardens should preserve, champion and enhance natural habitats, while also actively measuring and reducing their carbon and water footprints.

Natural plant community, colonizing a disused railway line.

Learning from Nature

Observations of natural areas, such as wildflower-rich footpaths, reveal that nature naturally favours density of planting. Natural plant communities are filled with plants that touch and tangle, embrace and scramble, lean and support each other. Further investigation reveals that these plantings are often part of a larger whole and have clearly defined layers. These include natural ground-cover layers, herbaceous layers, shrub layers and, ultimately, small trees and ones with larger canopies. Dense plantings such as these offer significant environmental impacts. They offer a dense supply of nectar and pollen, cover for amphibious life and invertebrates, shade and seclusion for nesting birds and so have a positive impact on the natural world.

This natural environment is significantly different to the principles that are often advocated within traditional gardening books, which often advocate more organised or regimented plantings. Importance is placed on accurate plant spacing to ensure that each plant has optimum light levels and space to regulate relative humidity. Plantings created to these traditional rules and principles often result in high-maintenance strategies, as the required light and space between plants encourages weeds and other spontaneous plants to compete. As many horticulturists are aware,

Dense plant communities offer a wide range of ecosystem services.

bare soil grows weeds. Or, as Aristotle put it, 'Horror vacui' — nature abhors a vacuum.

Implementing the principles of the environmental pillar and considering plantings as part of the wider ecosystem could inform a different approach. Local plant communities could be surveyed to identify natural planting densities, these can then be considered along with the more formal specifications, for example the planting of herbaceous perennials at seven or nine plants per square metre. Nature would suggest the use of higher planting densities, which mimic natural layering. These plantings will shade soil, reduce evaporation of water, provide dense pollen and nectar sources, and cover. Claudia West of Phyto Studio in Virginia in the USA is one of the leading voices in the developing field of ecological plantings. West takes this concept to its logical conclusion by suggesting that the plants themselves should be our mulch. Other leading experts in this field, such as Patrick McMillan, the Garden Director at Heronswood Garden in Washington, USA, describes this approach to planting as filling every gap — 'filling every space with useful plants that work for a living, selecting plants that not only meet our aesthetic need, but which also promote, enhance and enable biodiversity.'

Retraining Our Eyes

Managing gardens along sustainable principles and applying concepts such as layered ecological plantings will naturally give our gardens a different aesthetic, which will be challenging to some visitors. Those who come to a garden expecting to see perfect lawns, which are freshly mown and striped, will be challenged by that lawn being filled with wildflowers. Part of the role of the garden owner or manager is to gently challenge, to explain, to interpret what the visitor sees.

The visitor who is appalled that the lawn is filled with weeds may assume that this is the result of funding cuts, or that the staff are lazy and no longer care. Eyes can be retrained through education. Tilden, the father of modern interpretation, proposed that the purpose of interpretation is to share our passions with those of the visitor. Reviewing the ecosystem services that a formal lawn provides, against the aesthetic advantages and the ecosystem services that an ecological lawn filled with wildflowers provides, can explain the underlying motivation. The eyes of the visitor can then be retrained, from seeking assurance for viewing the anticipated striped grass, to viewing the dozens of bumblebees working the flowers.

This retraining of eyes is fundamental if people are to understand and to care about sustainably managed gardens. Explanations that the greenflies on the roses have been deliberately left to provide a food source for blue tits and provides a more natural experience for the visitor is another example of how eyes, and hearts, can be changed.

A key challenge in this process is that often the most significantly biodiverse areas of gardens are the very spaces that lack aesthetic charm. Areas of hard standing, filled with weeds, surrounded by nettles and brambles, are often important sites for moths, butterflies, insects and wild birds. The challenge is to create areas that offer rich habitat, food and water sources, with the visual appeal that the visitor requires. Creating multifunctional spaces that meet both of these requirements is one of the most significant challenges for those involved in garden and landscape design.

The sustainable gardener can keep abreast of this new thinking through visits to leading gardens, through watching YouTube videos and channels from reliable sources, through following stories on Instagram and attending meetings, seminars and conferences. These practices allow the curation of knowledge.

The implantation of the key concepts discussed results in the development of concepts such as best practice, which should inform all aspects of a garden's management. It includes the design of new garden areas, the application of new water-management strategies or the measurement of nectar provision from different wildflowers to inform species' selection. Organisations such as the Botanical Gardens, Plantlife, the Royal Society for the Protection of Birds, the Royal Horticultural Society, Plant Network or the Hardy Plant Society are useful sources of reliable information.

Standing on the Shoulders of Giants

Sir Isaac Newton stated, 'If I have seen further, it is by standing upon the shoulders of giants'. The sustainable gardening movement stands on the shoulders of many organisations that pioneered new approaches to gardening.

The organic gardening movement introduced many to the fundamental importance of soil health. Following the publication of seminal works, such as Rachel Carson's *Silent Spring*, it highlighted the impacts of synthetic pesticides, herbicides and fertilizers.

The wildlife gardening movement embraces many of the characteristics and principles of sustainable gardening. Sustainable gardening, however, takes this concept further to include the wider impacts that plants and gardens have on the local environment and on people. It also asks the gardener to consider the environmental impact of every input to the garden. These impacts can be far away, where the product is sourced, mined and manufactured. They can also be significant close by.

Permaculture, which is described by its founders as being to produce 'consciously designed landscapes which mimic the patterns and relationships found in nature, while yielding an abundance of food, fibre and energy for the provision of local needs', tends to focus on productive growing spaces, rather than the wider creation of a range of habitat types and the well-being of all people in the supply chain.

The sustainable gardening movement has taken the essence of many differing approaches to garden management and reviewed them against the three pillars of sustainability. The aim of sustainable gardening is to build on their pioneering work and take it further.

Questions	✓ ×
1. Are inputs to the garden evaluated to maximise the impact of people in the supply chain?	
2. Are inputs to the garden evaluated to minimise their negative environmental footprint?	
3. Are inputs, such as water, measured to establish a water footprint?	
4. Are human-powered tools favoured over fossil fuel-powered tools?	
5. Is the garden designed to create a range of habitats?	
6. Does the garden have a measurable impact on the local environment?	
7. Are plants sourced and grown locally to reduce their carbon footprint?	
8. Is rainwater harvested?	
9. Do hard surfaces drain sustainably to avoid the risk of flooding to neighbouring properties?	
10. Is all timber used from renewable, certified, well-managed woodlands?	

Ten Key Questions

The 'Questions' list provides an opportunity to apply some of the principles discussed and to establish a benchmark of sustainability.

The New Way to Garden

The new way to garden involves:

• Making a large number of small decisions.
• Measuring and evaluating.
• Researching and implementing best practice.

There are few definitive answers or rules that can be applied in every garden, as every garden is uniquely connected to its own ecosystem. In the absence of definitive rules, the sustainable gardener requires a tool to allow them to critically evaluate the impacts of every input and every intervention to allow the making of a million appropriate decisions.

This book proposes a new way of thinking. The new way to garden.

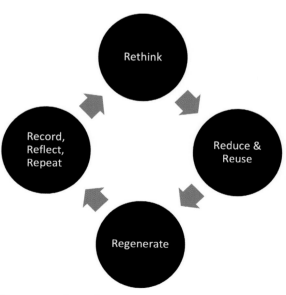

The new way to garden; a new model to inform sustainable decision-making.

Case Study: Sprint Mill Garden

Sprint Mill Garden in Cumbria is managed using ecological and sustainable principles. The garden includes woodland, natural meadow plantings and productive growing spaces. Owner Edward Acland defines their approach to garden management as 'Guardening'. Gardeners are the ultimate guardians of the environment and so the creation of habitat, and gardening using human-powered tools and equipment, are at the heart of this principle.

Sprint Mill is open by appointment. It is described by the National Garden Scheme as an: 'Unorthodox organically run garden, the wild and natural alongside provision of owners' fruit, vegetables and firewood. Idyllic riverside setting, 5 acres to explore including a wooded riverbank with hand-crafted seats. Large vegetable and soft fruit area, following no dig and permaculture principles. Hand tools prevail.'

Sprint Mill Garden, Cumbria.

Garden owner, Edward Acland, demonstrating a human-powered compost shredder.

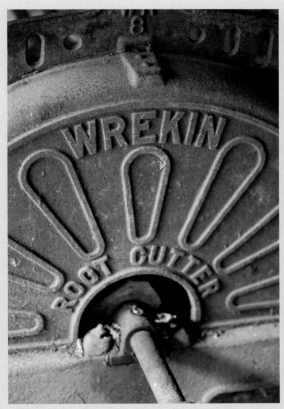

The 'Wrekin Root Cutter', which is still in use as a compost shredder.

A productive, no-dig garden, run on permaculture principles.

Sprint Mill, an 1840s felting mill, the windows boast 968 panes of glass. The mill is set on the banks of the river Sprint.

The river Sprint, which supports a wide range of species.

Rethink

The toolkit starts with the process of rethinking or reviewing new developments or interventions. This process involves asking a series of questions. The answers, while personal and only appropriate to the garden in question, should be recorded to allow later review and critical analysis.

Examples of the range of rethink questions include:

- What is the aim of this intervention?
- What is the latest thinking with regard to this intervention?
- What are the negative environmental impacts?
- What are the positive impacts?
- Is the overall result of this impact net positive?

An example of rethinking may be the planned actions and interventions required when blackfly is spotted on the extension growth on some shrubs. Training and lived experience suggest that a spray is required, perhaps a benign, organic product. Rethinking involves questioning and ranking possible responses. The aim of the intervention is not necessarily to kill the blackfly, it is to ensure plant health. Are the numbers of blackflies present, a critical risk to plant health? The next stage in rethinking is to investigate how other gardens or lead organisations are tackling this problem, if indeed it is a problem. Is monitoring sufficient? What are the negative impacts of intervention? Would the removal of the blackfles remove an important food source for wild birds at a time of the year when they are feeding young? What are the positive impacts of control, will flowering be enhanced? Is the overall control of blackflies that are not causing a significant plant health risk, but which remove a vital food source within the garden food chain, net positive?

The same thought process could be applied to a proposed new patio area. What is the aim of the area: to allow people to congregate, to create an alfresco dining area, to be able to find a spot to unwind with a glass of wine? What is the lowest impact way of creating an area to meet these needs? Can repurposed or recycled materials be used? Can the garden furniture be recycled or repurposed? Can the paving be laid with small gaps to allow water to percolate when there is a rainfall event to prevent run off or overwhelming drains? What is the minimum reasonable size of the paved area? Can paving be replaced with gravel or with plantings to soften the surface and add ecosystem services? What are the negative environmental impacts of the space – perhaps clusters of containers that require growing media and water, or the use of cement and the associated carbon release? What are the positive impacts? The edges of the paved area provide ecosystem services, the permeable surface will reduce flood risk, the materials are reused/repurposed/recycled. Other positive impacts relate to the people using the space and the creation of a market for repurposed materials.

When rethinking, the most interesting and profound answers often come from the questions we have not asked.

Tell Me What You Want, What You Really, Really Want…

The American politician and businessman Donald Rumsfeld is famous for stating:

As we know, there are known knowns; there are things we know we know. We also know there are known unknowns; that is to say we know there are some things we do not know. But there are also unknown unknowns — the ones we don't know we don't know.

It is the unknown unknowns that are a challenge to rethinking. To the person who knows only of the existence of paving and gravel as ways of creating hard surfacing, decking is an unknown unknown. Rethinking allows the discovery of unknown unknowns. To illustrate this point, the plantings around the new Hillside Centre for Horticultural Science at RHS Garden Wisley, include a model wildlife garden. In early late spring and early summer this garden is a sea of colour, with wildflowers of every description. The wildflowers in turn attract a wide range of wildlife, including many species of bumblebee, damsel fly and butterfly. During a visit the author overheard visitors making a variety of comments, including, 'this is it', 'this is what I want my garden to be', 'this could be my best garden', 'I didn't know you could make gardens like this'. We are often limited by the boundaries of our knowledge and lived experience. Rethinking can be a revolutionary act.

High-density plantings of wildflowers at RHS Garden Wisley, showcasing a more sustainable approach to garden management.

Higher density plantings allow plants to intertwine, as they would in nature.

Wildflowers offer the opportunity to re-wild gardens.

Reduce and Reuse

The second part of the toolkit involves evaluating all inputs to identify if materials can be reduced or reused. Examples of the range of rethink questions include:

- Is this a material that can be sourced or grown within the garden?
- Can other materials be reused or repurposed to provide this function?
- Can the environmental impacts of sourcing this material be reduced?
- Can the quantities of materials and inputs be reduced?
- Are there alternatives with lower carbon and water footprints?

Areas of still water with aquatic plants provide habitat for damsel flies.

This part of the process develops a layered approach to the sustainable thought process.

A simple example could be the requirements to provide plant supports for the cultivation of peas and beans within a productive growing space. Garden canes that are grown and shipped from China are often a first choice for beans, with plastic netting supported by canes used for peas. Applying the principles of reduce and reuse would question this approach. Could prunings be used to provide pea sticks and beanpoles? If not, could small areas be planted with hazel to provide this material from within the garden?

Mulch made from wheat straw. Chopped *Miscanthus* would produce a similar product, which would be topped up annually.

A further example could relate to the practice of mulching. Mulches are used to reduce weed growth and to maintain moisture levels in the soil. From a sustainability perspective they also provide habitat and a food source for microorganisms, which decompose and break down the mulch into humic substances. These substances bind with mineral particles in the soil, causing the formation of soil crumbs, which are a vital component of a healthy soil.

It, therefore, would not be appropriate to consider reduce and reuse in this instance. However, these mulching materials are often bought in. They can arrive on pallets, with plastic pallet wrap, in plastic sacks, delivered by a transportation system that releases large quantities of carbon. When one delves further into the collection of organic material, its processing and handling also involves the release of carbon. The reduce and reuse concept is very applicable to these situations. For example, all of the carbon release and plastic use could be eliminated if the mulch was produced within the garden. *Miscanthus* is a fast-growing grass, which is often used as a biofuel. If space allowed within the garden, a stand of *Miscanthus* could be grown for cutting and shredding to produce high-quality, garden-grown mulch.

Regenerate

At their best, sustainable gardens offer regenerative services. These services can include the creation of habitat, with a resulting increase in biodiversity, along with the regenerative effects that these spaces have on communities and the wellness and mental health of those who engage with such spaces.

Examples of the range of regenerative questions include:

- Does the garden support the creation of priority habitats identified in the UK biodiversity action plan?
- Does the garden support priority species identified in the UK biodiversity action plan?
- Does the garden sequester carbon?
- Does the purchase of goods and services offer regeneration in other communities?
- Does the garden engage with citizen science projects as part of its regenerative mission?

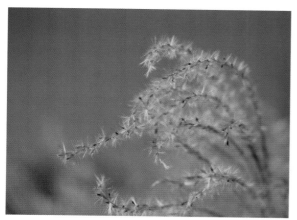

Miscanthus, a fast-growing grass, adds colour, volume and movement to plantings. It can be used to create garden-grown mulches.

A key aspect of a sustainable garden is the measurable impact that it has on the wider world. These impacts can be considered as being either direct or indirect. Direct regenerative impacts would include, for example, the application of mulches to soil to regenerate the soil ecosystem, or the cultivation of plants that provide habitat and berries to produce food for wild birds and small mammals. Hard-landscaping surfaces can be used to divert water into bog gardens, which can help with the regeneration of this habitat type. The indirect regenerative impacts could include the social and economic impacts of our buying decisions. When considering the materials for a new driveway or hardstanding area, initial thoughts may consider rethinking the purpose of such areas and the reduction and reuse of materials. It may, however, be that to match existing surfaces a material such as Indian sandstone is considered. There are obvious sustainability challenges with this material, including the impacts of quarries on the environment in India, the environmental footprint of shipping the sandstone and its wider carbon footprint. Other significant concerns could include the reported fact that one-fifth of the workforce in India's quarries are children, some as young as six years old. Bonded labour, where people are forced to work to pay off a debt, is rife. Sustainable suppliers such as Marshalls have responded to these serious social issues by launching product lines such as 'fairstone', where they audit the supply chain, do not tolerate child labour and ensure that the stone itself is of high quality with the minimum environmental impact.

The concept of regeneration can be considered in other more mundane areas. Many gardens use a spring application of pelleted chicken manure. Apart from the obvious impacts of packaging and transportation, an investigation of several manufacturers' websites failed to identify the source of the manure or the conditions under which the chickens were being reared. This leads to interesting ethical questions: if we insist, for animal welfare issues, that our eggs from the supermarket or that are served in our cafés are free range, do we carry out similar checks when sourcing pelleted chicken manure?

Case Study: Rethink, Reduce, Reuse

A community group has sought to enhance their community green through the purchase and the planting of a row of large plastic pots, placed inside twenty-five half-barrels. These are planted with spring and summer bedding plants to create year-round interest. The flowers cultivated in the barrels offer nectar for pollinators and their leaves are food sources for caterpillars.

Rethinking could include a fundamental review of the aim of the plantings: would the creation of a permanent planting in the ground offer the same impact?

Reduce and reuse thinking could be applied to measure water, growing media, young plant and peat inputs, to strengthen the case for planting in the ground as a more sustainable option.

Twenty-five large barrels, filled with 3,500ltr of growing media, requiring a high-water input and refilling twice a year. Rethinking may offer a more sustainable solution.

Top Tip

The production of virgin growing media produces a considerable environmental footprint. Material is sourced, transported, processed, screened, bagged, transported to the wholesaler and again to the retailer.

Traditional thinking suggests always using fresh, new, sterile growing media, with reuse being considered bad practice. However, many are now rethinking and re-evaluating this approach. The concept of refreshing growing media is gaining traction, where the plant health risks are considered along with the environmental impacts of using virgin material.

A recent development has been the potential use of hot-composted green waste to produce the base for a growing media, created at least in part by material produced within the garden. This concept is further discussed in Chapter 8.

Record, Reflect, Repeat

The final part of the toolkit allows us to record the intentional and unintentional impacts of our new approaches to gardens management. It allows us to measure the impact of our planting choices or our hard-landscape installations.

Examples of the range of record, reflect, repeat questions include:

- Have there been positive intentional impacts?
- Have there been positive unintentional impacts?
- Have there been unexpected negative impacts?
- Could the process be improved?
- Could this thinking be applied to other garden areas?

Recording could include engagement with citizen science projects, such as the RSPB's Big Garden Birdwatch, which allows the measurement over time of the impacts that garden areas can have on wild bird populations. Other projects include Plantlife's No Mow May and Every Flower Counts, or Butterfly Conservation's Big Butterfly Count.

Counting birds, wildflowers, butterflies and wildlife present within gardens provides a benchmark to inform and measure the garden's sustainability journey. These data sets then allow projects and initiatives to be evaluated on their measurable regenerative impacts.

Garden trees can be added to websites such as treezilla, a project started in 2013 between the Open University, Forest Research and Treeconomics. This project helps with tree, pest and disease identification, and quantifies ecosystem services, such as quantities of run-off water avoided, along with measures of air quality improvement and carbon sequestration.

The recording of data, the review of initiatives and interventions on wildlife and on other metrics, such as plant growth and flowering, inform decisions relating to whether to repeat interventions, or to discontinue, modify and amend them.

Top Tip

Ethical Trading Initiative member organisations seek to ensure that their products are not made by:

- The 3 billion people living on less than $2 a day.
- One of the 218 million children forced into work.
- One of the 6,000 people who die every day from work-related accidents and diseases.

Top Tip

Citizen science projects are most effective when carried out on the same day (or in the same weather conditions), at the same time each year.

It is good practice to create a simple graph to chart the population variances year on year.

It is also useful to read the findings of the citizen science projects to benchmark the garden against others in the region and nationally.

CHAPTER 2

IT ALL STARTS WITH GOOD DESIGN DECISIONS

Thinking about design is hard but not thinking about it can be disastrous.

Ralph Caplan

Sustainable garden design has evolved rapidly over recent years. The first sustainable designs contained limited elements, such as the specification of repurposed timber elements for an arbour or proposed naturalistic plantings for pollinators. These sustainable features were often viewed in a similar way to locating generosity within the design. The concept of locating generosity within the design is often used by designers to add magic, or generous touches in one aspect of the design. A garden that is being designed to a budget may have restrained hard landscaping, but the generosity in the design is applied to the exuberant plantings. As sustainability has evolved, it is increasingly being located in the primary motivations that inform the core design process.

These primary motivations could include:

- How the garden meets the needs of the client.
- How the garden interacts with the wider ecosystem/environment in which it sits.
- How the impacts of a changing climate inform design decisions.
- How hard surfaces can be sustainable and serve ecological functions.
- How waste can be reduced through repurposing and recycling materials.
- How procurement supports fairness and equity in the supply chain.
- How carbon and water footprints are managed.

Meeting the Needs of the Client

A key design skill is involved in receiving and responding to the brief, in questioning, probing and gently challenging, in suggesting and testing the water to establish clear boundaries and to prioritise key criteria that are non-negotiables with the client. This can allow natural discussions about wildlife and pollinators, alongside discussions about the way the client may want to use and interact with the space.

These discussions often highlight requirements relating to:

- Child-friendly spaces.
- Preferred colour palette.
- Preference for formal or informal style.
- Discussions relating to maintenance input.
- Minimalist or other design concepts.
- The inclusion of productive growing areas.
- The requirements for seasonal interest.

Cottage gardens create flower-led, productive spaces, whereas potagers create vegetable-led productive spaces.

Each of these requirements can be considered from a sustainability perspective. Child-friendly could be interpreted as areas that lead to natural play, and which introduce the child, in a safe and considered manner, to mud, insects and wildlife. Other aspects such as colour palette, seasonality and formality/informality can be considered through the specification of plantings that act as functioning ecosystems. These plantings provide habitat and food sources for wildlife, they enhance the soil and, if containing woody plants, play a role in carbon sequestration. Careful adherence to 'right plant, right place', results in minimal site amelioration, and provides a planting that has minimal needs for inputs of water or synthetic fertilizers.

When creating new, specialist garden areas, sustainability should be at the heart of every decision. When considering, for example, the development of new productive growing spaces, key questions could include: the design of nursery areas to allow the production of plants on site; the provision of areas that are plastic free; the advocation of minimal cultivation; or the provision of on-site composting. These areas can be enhanced by actions such as the cultivation of comfrey for the production of nutrient-rich feeds, which can replace synthetic fertilizers.

Provision of Ecosystem Services

Within the field of sustainable garden design, an ecosystem can be considered to be dynamic communities of plants, animals and microorganisms that interact as functional units with the non-living aspects of the garden. Ecosystem services take this principle and consider the benefits that people derive from nature that both support and fulfil human life. Examples could include: cultural ecosystem services, the creation of beauty and the

Nutrient-rich feeds can be made from *Symphytum officinale* (Comfrey) to replace synthetic fertilizers in gardens.

Checklist for Designers

- Does the garden sequester carbon?
- Have functioning ecosystems been created?
- Have habitats been created?
- Does the garden have a low carbon footprint?
- Does the garden have a low water footprint?
- Have plastic-based products been reduced or eliminated?
- Are existing materials reused or repurposed?
- Is the garden net positive?

Rosehips add interest and colour to late summer gardens.

Rosehips also provide a useful food source for garden birds.

natural health benefits of being surrounded by nature. They also include the provision of cover, shelter, roosting and nesting spaces that plants may provide, which benefit nature, which in turn benefits people. Other ecosystem services could include the provision of food for both humans and wildlife, or the provision of shade, the filtering of air and noise reduction.

A four-stage process is often used to evaluate the provision of ecosystem services:

1. A definition of aims and the scope of the project or design.

2. The identification and prioritisation of ecosystem services in the design process. This includes decisions such as which services are most important — regionally, nationally or to the client.

3. The development of key decisions and metrics to ensure efficacy. This could include the financial investment, undertaking a cost—benefit analysis or the assessment of environmental risks and priorities.
4. The assessment of outcomes over both the short and long term, to inform any mitigations that may be required, and to inform the approach taken with future projects.

To consider this concept further, grassed areas are often viewed as problematic within sustainable garden management. They do, however, provide important ecosystem services. These include the provision of play areas for children, cultural services, such as enhancing aesthetics in setting off borders, or the provision of negative space within the design. These grassed areas can also contain lawn weeds or spontaneous plants, which provide nectar and pollen, and attract pollinating insects into the garden, which not only contribute to the overall ecosystem within the garden but also connect people with nature. These positive attributes are then balanced against the more problematic aspects of managing grassed areas. These include the requirement to be mown, which often involves the direct or indirect burning of fossil fuels, the use of fertilizers, the production of which contributes to global warming, or the use of herbicides to control weed species. The aim of the sustainable gardener is to boost the ecosystem services and reduce the negative impacts to create net-positive garden areas.

Spirit of Place

To create a garden that sits correctly within the local environment often involves researching a concept known as Spirit of Place. This process includes developing a deep understanding of the area in which the garden is to be created, allowing the development of a unique design proposal that reflects a number of key criteria:

- The extent to which the design proposal celebrates the unique aspects of the place.
- Respecting and valuing how people have related to this space through the ages.
- The impacts of documented references to the place in, for example, song, fable, poetry, writings or paintings.

- The impact of previous historical designs on new proposals.

Impacts of Climate Change

Climate scientists are suggesting that impacts of climate change on gardens will include warmer temperatures, with increased prevalence of storms, high winds, significant rainfall events and extended periods of drought. Sustainable garden designers are responding to such scenarios by designing gardens that mitigate as many of these effects as possible. This could include the provision of shaded patio areas to reduce the impacts of high temperatures, stormscaping practices that can include the pollarding of trees to avoid damage from high winds and the provision of rain gardens to hold water and to reduce the risk of flooding caused by run-off.

Hard Surfaces

The specification of hard surfaces is often considered to be problematic within sustainable garden design. Key considerations can include:

- The repair, repointing and refurbishment of walls and surfaces.
- The repurposing and reuse of hard materials within the garden.
- The procurement of previously used materials from architectural salvage.
- The procurement of local stone and gravel products to reduce carbon footprints.
- The procurement of ethically sourced product, for example Marshalls' fairstone products.
- The contribution of hard surfaces to sustainable drainage goals.

Further considerations could include the use of hard surfaces to provide ecosystem services to include:

- The use of environmental impact assessments to inform decisions.
- The inclusion of planting pockets within walls, where appropriate.
- The preservation of habitat when repointing and refurbishing.

- The use of hard surfaces in rainwater harvesting.
- The use of lime mortar to allow habitat for masonry bees.
- The specification of planting within joints as transitions to planted areas.
- The lifting of paving slabs to provide planting spaces.
- The role of raised beds in the cultivation of food crops.
- The provision of habitat, for example bat boxes or wild bird nesting boxes.
- The provision of cultural ecosystem services, such as aesthetics and relaxation.

When the designer is involved in interpreting the client brief, they have to consider the relationship between the soft and hard landscaping elements. From a sustainability perspective, plants offer the greatest environmental return, as previously stated. The hard landscaped areas are essential to allow for ease of movement through the garden or to enable the creation of seating areas, and while these do offer ecosystem services, these are outweighed on a metre-by-metre basis by soft landscaping. Balance is required.

Transition Zones

Garden designers often create what are referred to as transition zones to allow a garden to flow and to integrate the hard and soft landscaping.

A house is, almost always, the largest, most dominant hard feature. It is formal and dominates. The garden, however, may have softer and more flowing elements. There is a perennial issue of how these two

Hard works can add charm to the garden, especially if made from recycled stone.

Artist Sarah Walton sculpts birdbaths on green oak bases, which add a soft yet sculptural ecosystem service to gardens.

A seating area, included in the Welcome to Yorkshire Garden designed by Mark Gregory at the 2019 Chelsea Flower Show.

The architect, Edwin Lutyens, designed the circular steps at Great Dixter Garden; these bring the house to the garden, and the garden to the house.

Cellular grassed paving systems, allow grass and wildflowers to be cultivated in areas where vehicles are used.

elements can sit comfortably together. This is where the concept of transition zones can be applied.

A patio or terrace is used to take the hard features of the house into the garden; while plantings, pots, troughs and containers bring the soft features of the garden to the house. Transition zones allow these often-contradictory elements to sit together comfortably. These zones can be important areas that increase the density of planting within a garden but can also be problematic if they use high volumes of growing media to fill pots or large volumes of water.

Cooling and Shading

Site appraisals or the position of the house often determine areas that are appropriate for development as patios or relaxation zones. These areas are often chosen as they are in full sun. However, the impact of climate change may result in increased intensity and duration of sun, through reduced cloud cover. It may, therefore, be wise to consider the planting of a tree that can cast a light, dappled shade or to plant climbers to help cool the walls of the house.

Waste-Reduction Strategies

Some sustainable garden designers are now using the number of skips leaving a site as a metric to measure the sustainability of their design. Waste materials from garden builds result in emissions from transport and can result in further emissions from incineration or from landfill, none of which are desirable. A paradigm shift in thinking may be required to consider rotten timber as a valuable raw material to create habitat piles or hibernacula, rather than being a waste material. Traditional thinking may suggest the use of virgin hard landscaping materials; however, the reuse or relaying of hard materials can dramatically reduce both cost and the carbon footprint of the garden. (Garden designers and installers should be aware that reuse and repurposing can have impacts on warranties and should seek advice as required.)

Kaizen: The Art of Improvement

The concept of kaizen, a business philosophy that originated in Japan, can be applied in the process of designing and installing sustainable gardens. Kaizen emphasises that whether one is looking at increased productivity, the elimination of waste or improvement in quality control, success often comes from the implementation of many tiny, micro-changes, rather than one sweeping reform of the system.

The concepts considered within this chapter from the ecosystem services provided by lawns to the reuse of materials are examples of how the principles of kaizen are being woven into the thought process. What tiny changes would enhance ecosystem services? What tiny changes would reduce the negative environmental impacts of lawn maintenance? Developing this thinking as a permanent process that is applied to every aspect of garden design, build and maintenance can lead to considerable change over time.

Claudia West is one of the leading figures in sustainable garden and landscape design. She is Principal at Phyto Studio, who specialise in bridging the gap between horticulture and ecology, with a vision of creating plant-covered cities.

When asked about the realities of designing sustainable gardens, West explains:

It is hard. You have to see the opportunities that are hidden deep within the project. You have to be relentless; you have to think bigger. You have to keep the client on board, you have to elevate everyone, the contractor the nursery, the gardeners who will care for the landscape. We have to continually teach and elevate these people.

Kaizen is an effective tool in continually teaching, elevating, explaining, challenging, and in the relentless pursuit of sustainable design.

The New Way to Garden Toolkit

The new toolkit that was proposed in Chapter 1 involves a four-stage process to inform sustainable-gardening decisions:

- Rethink.
- Reduce and reuse.
- Regenerate.
- Record, reflect, repeat.

Claudia West, Principal, Phyto Studio.

West designs gardens as working ecosystems.

These key considerations can further develop the thought process regarding the design of sustainable gardens.

Rethinking

This aspect can be initiated as soon as the results of the formal site appraisal process are known. This process involves assessing the site against a number of key criteria, which can include:

- The general character of the landscape, for example is this a woodland garden or a courtyard garden?
- The climate, the rainfall, the relation of the site to the sun and prevailing winds.
- Existing buildings.
- The position of boundaries and their nature.
- The position of key existing features, including ponds and streams.
- The characteristics of the soil.
- Underground and overhead structures and services.

There are also countless minor considerations, which include:

- Frost pockets or shaded cool areas, often the last places winter snow will melt.
- Rain shadows caused by buildings, which are often at the bases of walls.
- Sheltered areas within the site.

Traditionally, site appraisals were carried out to inform the alteration of levels, ground works required to position and install patios and other hard features, and to inform the design and installation of drainage systems. The findings also inform soil amelioration or replacement practices that might be required to make the site appropriate to the plant selections.

Rethinking this process allows the consideration of how the design can be implemented with minimal mitigations. As Claudia West suggests, 'We have to see the opportunities in every project'. This requires the designer to ask, what design can be developed that requires the lightest touch on the site, that utilizes unique damper areas, that celebrates slopes or that chooses plants that thrive in dry, sandy soils.

This process of rethinking, of applying the principles of minimal intervention, of using a palette of plants that are suited to the unimproved site, of providing ecological habitats and ecosystem services, requires fundamental changes to the design process. Best practice can be researched through the review of the latest scientific papers, published in peer-reviewed journals, reference to books or visiting other gardens to see how they are weaving the threads of sustainable thinking into their practices. In the UK, this could include visits to National Trust properties, the RHS gardens at Hyde Hall, Rosemoor, Wisley, Harlow Carr and Bridgewater. On a more domestic scale, this can include visits to 'Yellow Book' gardens, which offer unique perspectives of how people have overcome site limitations in the creation of their gardens.

To gain the maximum benefit from visits to gardens, it is wise to view these as research trips with the purpose of solving a pre-determined range of issues. Suitable questions could include:

- How has the owner worked with the existing soil?
- How is the soil managed?
- How have they reduced traffic noise?
- How have they celebrated and used local materials?
- How do the plantings support local wildlife?

The concept of designing gardens that do good and that have a positive and measurable effect on wildlife can, for example, be informed through visits to local wildlife trust nature reserves, to research and understand the pressures on local wildlife. Such investigation can be used to identify that a particular species of butterfly is under threat. Further research could reveal that a particular rare wildflower is ideal both for egg-laying and also as an important source of nectar. This knowledge can then inform some of our later planting decisions and help to meet the goal of creating a garden that does good and that deeply connects with the local ecosystem.

Researching and rethinking other key components of the garden design can apply this same thought process. Vertical barriers are a good example of where rethinking and research can lead to informed decisions. Walls and fencing are often specified as vertical boundaries as they are relatively quick and easy to install, they look clean and tidy and do the job.

Cardamine pratense is an important host for the orange tip butterfly.

Research will identify the more sustainable options, such as selecting the materials with the lowest carbon footprint for the construction of a wall (from the quarrying for raw materials to the energy consumed in manufacture and distribution). Fences can be specified to be made from Forest Stewardship Council timber. The most interesting sustainable gardening answers come from the questions we have not asked. Walls, even when built from reclaimed materials, have high carbon footprints. The carbon emissions associated with the transport of even the most sustainable timber negates much of the environmental benefits. Hedges on the other hand offer a much lower carbon and water footprint, form soft green boundaries, create habitats, provide ecosystem services and sequester carbon. The combination of these factors makes them a more sustainable solution. A limitation is that they take time to establish. Fedges in this instance may be the most sustainable solution, combining the instant convenience of a fence, with the environmental benefits of a hedge.

To minimise the water footprint of gardens the designer can specify, where appropriate, field-grown, bare-root plants, which often have a fraction of the water footprint of container-grown plants. Smaller plants can be specified, as these too have reduced water footprints. Specifying drought-tolerant plants would mitigate the need to install irrigation systems, which are often made from plastics.

The reduction of the water footprint of intensively cultivated garden areas, such as productive growing settings should be considered. This could involve the installation of water collection systems, water storage systems, and water-wise irrigation systems.

Reducing

One of our key sustainable garden management principles is to reduce the negative footprint that gardens can make on the planet.

While gardens and the world of horticulture are often seen as green and ecological, they can very easily be hugely environmentally damaging. They can use excessive and unsustainable quantities of:

- Water.
- Fossil fuel.
- Plastic.
- Quarried material.
- Fertilizer.
- Peat.

The manufacture of fertilizer releases greenhouse gasses and contributes to climate change.

By considering each of these aspects in turn, we can identify ways to reduce these negative impacts. We have already discussed ways within the design and installation process to reduce water footprints. The International Fertilizer Industry Association have published data that indicate that fertilizer manufacture accounts for approximately 1 per cent of global greenhouse gas emissions. When one adds in the associated nitrous oxide emissions from applying this fertilizer, then the total increases to 2.5 per cent of the global total. Yara International, who manufacture fertilizers, state on their website that the average 100 per cent carbon footprint from using a nitrogen fertilizer is 5.6kg CO_2-eqv per kg of applied N.

The gravel used in gardens has to be extracted from quarries, washed and then transported with considerable carbon emissions, and the hugely detrimental impacts of peat extraction on the environment are well documented and thankfully have resulted in an impending ban on peat usage, first for the amateur market and then for professional horticulturists.

Regenerate

The next layer of thinking in the design of a sustainable garden is that of regeneration.

Is the garden design proposal regenerative? Does the proposal:

- Regenerate and restore plant communities?
- Regenerate and restore animal communities?
- Regenerate the unseen ecology of the soil?
- Reduce the need for soil disturbance?
- Include a recycling/composting area?
- Include the use of permanent plantings?
- Embrace concepts such as companion planting?
- Benefit the wider community?

Recording, Reflecting, Repeat and Learning from Other Designers

This process starts with ascertaining what is present on the site at the start of the process. What range of plants is on-site? What wildlife calls the garden home? What ecosystems are supported? To answer these questions involves carrying out simple surveys. The result of these surveys should be drivers in the design process. Are the plants present ecologically significant? How many species of wild bird visit the garden? Are there bats, newts or hedgehogs that are using the garden? Before the designer even considers removing overgrown vegetation and replacing it, fundamental questions should be asked. What is here? What is significant? What should be treasured and enhanced?

Reflective practice requires the designer to stop and to consider the intended decisions and directions, asking the question: is this wise? Visiting others who have made similar design decisions and learning the important lessons that can be learnt through their experiences, involves the development of communities of practice where professionals can come together to meet, discuss, reflect, and hone best practice.

Case Study: RHS Garden Bridgewater

Many of the principles considered within this chapter, from the concepts of identifying wildlife habitats under threat, to reusing and repurposing materials, were at the heart of the development of the Royal Horticultural Society's fifth garden at Bridgewater.

- The garden is 62.3 hectares (154 acres) in size and opened to the public in May 2021.
- In 2016 and 2017 work started on recording, measuring and surveying the ecosystems present within the garden. The Royal Horticultural Society (RHS) website reveals just 282 plant taxa present at that time, with 42 bird species and a small number of bats newts and invertebrates. This established a base line, against which the impact of new plantings could be measured.
- Key ecological goals were established, with plants being chosen to complement the local area and to increase biodiversity, with specific reference to the RHS Plants for Pollinators initiative.
- The UK Biodiversity Action Plan highlights deciduous woodland and lowland fell and habitats that are at risk. This prompted the team at RHS Garden Bridgewater to add these to the list of habitats to be created within the garden. Other habitats created to become functioning ecosystems within Bridgewater are meadows, ponds and bog gardens.
- A large project was undertaken to establish Spirit of Place, to capture stories and lived experiences of people connected with the site over many years. The information gained through this initiative informed the design and development of the garden.

- One of the three pillars of sustainability identified in the introduction to this book is people. With the rising cost of housing, a growing rental market, people renting bedsit accommodation and other factors, outdoor space to garden is not always available. A key design feature of the garden was the provision of areas where members of the community can come and garden, share knowledge, experience and build a community and experience social inclusion.
- The garden has been designed with water management at its heart and adopts the principle of working with the site and nature, rather than against it. An example of this can be seen in the way water is managed on the site. Surface rainwater is collected, diverted through various habitats, swales and ditches to fill Ellesmere Lake, a decorative feature of the garden adjacent to the welcome building. From a more functional perspective, car parks drain into a detention pond, which can hold 24h of rainwater, thus preventing run-off and the risk of flooding to adjacent areas. Water harvested on site is used in irrigation.
- The build of the garden was managed to ensure materials were reused, recycled and repurposed as a key priority. When soil within the new productive growing area was shown to be contaminated, this was reused in decorative areas, with uncontaminated soil from these areas being used in the productive area. While this involved moving huge amounts of soil, the principle of reducing materials moving off site, and of reducing inputs, was put into practice.
- Materials unearthed during the build process were retained on site as useful resources. This initiative

evolved into the curation of bricks and other hard landscape features, which were then available in the repair and restoration of other areas, enhancing aesthetics and reducing the need for virgin materials. An example of this is the Worsley Delph Rock, sandstone of up to 20m (66ft) thick found on site. This was salvaged and then used to create the Chinese streamside garden.

- Low-carbon, ground-clearance strategies were used, including the use of six Berkshire pigs. These 'ground-clearance machines' were introduced to a new fenced-off area of the site, and almost immediately their heads went down and their snouts became ploughs, plants and their roots were eaten (with great delight) and returned to the soil as droppings.
- Ecologists were brought in to advise on habitat creation, for example, prior to de-silting a lake, the area was scoured for amphibians that could be rehoused to other ponds prior to the works being undertaken.

CHAPTER 3

SOIL: THE UNSEEN ECOSYSTEM

A mere 2 per cent increase in the carbon content of the planet's soils could offset 100 per cent of all greenhouse gas emissions going into the atmosphere.

Dr Rattan Lal, Professor of Soil Science,
Ohio State University

The etymology for the word human can be traced to the word humus, which is a building block of soil. This means that we can class human beings as soil beings.

The Sustainable Soils Alliance report on their website that:

- UK soils are being destroyed ten times faster than they are being created.
- UK soils store 10 billion tonnes of carbon in the form of organic matter. This equates to eighty years of greenhouse gas emissions.
- Intensive farming has resulted in UK soils losing 40—60 per cent of their organic carbon.

These statistics illustrate very clearly the importance of soil as a carbon sink, and the potential of soils to sequester carbon. Managing soils to maximise carbon capture, to enhance the unseen ecosystem present within soils and to meet plant requirements have resulted in the need to fundamentally review soil-management practices at every level of horticulture. Digging as a traditional technique involved in soil management has been shown to release carbon from the soil and disrupt the soil ecosystem. The use of fertilizers has been shown to have a significantly detrimental impact on the soil ecosystem. The use of these two practices must, therefore, at the very least be questioned, and possibly discontinued.

Understanding Soils

Soils and other growing media (composts used in container growing) provide the plant with a number of essential services. In their optimal state, they allow for the penetration of roots and so provide anchorage for plants. As the climate changes, with more significant weather events predicted, this role of providing anchorage is likely to become ever more important. Roots that are stunted by poor soil structure, high water tables, pans or other associated factors will not be able to penetrate deeply, and so the plant will be exposed to potential health risks, such as wind rock. It may be, as we move to a future with more extreme weather events, that the ability of a plant to root deeply will become one of the characteristics used in plant selection, with plant breeders adding such adaptations to their lists of desirable features along with flower colour, scent, enhanced seasons of interest and so on.

Plant roots require oxygen and so the soils have to provide the ability for gaseous exchange to allow a constant supply of oxygen. Plant roots also require a constant supply of water. The formation of soil, which provides optimum gaseous exchange and water supply to plants, can be witnessed through the topping-up of mulch. Mulching with organic material to a depth of 7cm (3in) is a standard horticultural practice in many situations. The mulch often requires topping-up annually, as it seems to disappear. Further investigation reveals that, while mulching material disappears as a physical presence, a dark staining can often be observed, especially in lighter, sandy soils. This staining is caused by humic substances that have been released due to the decomposition of the mulch by microorganisms. These humic substances are sticky and coat the rock particles within the soil or add volume to soil crumbs. This process is soil formation at work. These soil crumbs grow in volume and, as they grow, they are able to hold more water that is available to the plant. As they get larger, they split and produce smaller crumbs of soil, the gaps between these crumbs allowing for the diffusion of oxygen into the root zone. The humic substances are long-lasting and carbon-rich, explaining how this process sequesters carbon. It is thought that increasing the organic matter levels in soils in this manner could be a significant tool in slowing climate change.

Rainfall patterns are predicted to change as a result of climate change; these changes will result in soils having to cope with high levels of rainfall over short periods of time, accompanied by long periods during which there will be minimal rainfall. Plants require a consistent supply of water, both for cooling and for photosynthesis, which draws carbon out of the atmosphere. Plants also require water to enable them to take up the essential elements required for growth and the maintenance of health. Soils with strong crumb structures, and high levels of organic matter in the form of humic substances, are more able to meet this need than those with poor crumb structures and low levels of humic substances.

Fragile — Handle with Care

Garden-management practices have profound impacts on the crumb structure within soil. Walking on the soil while it is wet, the use of heavy machinery, such as lawnmowers, and the cultivation of soil, all

Twenty-eight per cent of arable soils in the UK are degraded, which reduces their potential to hold water and store carbon.

Deep mulching on a raised bed, formed from corten steel. Part of an endless pursuit to create habitat.

negatively impact on the crumb structure. Without careful management, soil can compact to become dense with limited air spaces. This has negative impacts on root growth and plant health as oxygen is no longer able to freely diffuse into the soil. Sustainable soil-management practices, such as mulching with organic materials, as has already been seen, can over a relatively short period of time correct many of these issues. The higher levels of organic matter, which is a food source for earthworms, nematodes and microorganisms, result in population increases. These organisms play a positive role in both crumb formation and the creation of drainage channels, which also aid in the diffusion of oxygen.

Compacted soils, which sometimes show surface cracking in periods of drought, can also shed water in periods of high rainfall, thus increasing run-off and risk of flooding. Soils with strong crumb structures allow the percolation of water through their profile and so reduce the risk of run-off and flooding.

Did You Know What Is In Just One Teaspoonful of Garden Soil?

There are more living organisms in one teaspoon of soil, than there are people on the planet.

Kathy Merrifield, a scientist who studied soil organisms at Oregon State University, is reported as explaining that a single teaspoon (1g) of rich garden soil can hold up to 1 billion bacteria, several metres of fungal filaments, several thousand protozoa and scores of nematodes.

Soil management should be considered as an important aspect of garden management. This includes positive practices such as mulching, but also the monitoring and prevention of damage. Many gardens that are open to the public have car parking situated in grassland under the cover of trees. Trees afford ecosystem services to the driver, offering shade to keep the car cool. This practice, however, compacts the soil under the trees, which can result in the roots being deprived of oxygen and root death. A process called air spading, where lances are inserted into the soil, which vibrate and pump a mix of air and organic material into the soil, are used to mitigate such circumstances with significant effect. Trees that are in decline often put on significant growth as their roots are able once again to respire and penetrate the soil, thus illustrating the importance of understanding the way that soils impact on plant growth.

Productive settings such as allotments often use raised beds as components of their soil management strategies. Permanent paths are created, avoiding the compaction caused by pedestrian and wheeled traffic. The process of raising soil levels also has negative impacts. It involves significant disruption to the soil ecosystem, with the associated release of carbon. The beds, being raised, are more resilient to the impacts of major rainfall events but are also more prone to drought conditions. This can lead to either a reduction in the range of crops that can be grown, or a potentially unsustainable use of water. The edges of raised beds are often made of plastic, an unsustainable material, or wood. Treated wood presents a risk of leachate affecting the soil ecosystem, or even contaminating food grown. The wood rots, and needs to be replaced using up raw materials, and also provides habitat for slugs and snails.

Terraforming Plants

Very few people involved in the management of gardens and designed landscapes would describe their soils as perfect. There is a wide range of products available that are sold as soil improvers. There is, however, significant evidence that plants, when left to their own devices, often ameliorate or significantly change the soil around them. One of the principles of sustainable soil-management is to support this process of terraforming. As an example, conifers often perform better in soils that are slightly acidic. As they grow, they drop pine needles and create a blanket or mulch around the roots. The pine needles are acidic. So, as this mulch breaks down and is incorporated into the soil, it acidifies the soil. Some gardens have reported that when acid-loving plants are planted, and fallen branches, needles and twigs are left in place to be integrated back into the soil through natural processes, the pH can be significantly more acid. Records indicate that soils that were pH 7.0 at planting, can change to pH 5.5 after a few years as a result of this process.

Other gardeners have reported that the structure (the arrangement of crumbs within the soil) can differ in various zones according to the plants grown, as indeed can the nutritional content of the soil in these zones. This has led to the establishment of 'chop n drop' as a principle of soil management. Herbaceous plants that have grown and finished flowering are left within such garden areas to provide attractive seed heads and to provide food and habitat to overwintering invertebrates. In the spring, the normal practice would be to prune the growth to ground level, and then compost it. With the 'chop n drop' model of management, the growth from herbaceous perennials is chopped to 200mm (8in) lengths and allowed to fall to the ground at the base of the plant. As this material rots, it returns to the soil essential elements that the plant had absorbed and encourages soil-development processes that favour the plant.

Sustainable garden management applies the principle of minimising necessary interventions. The removal of plant material for central composting does little to support this process of allowing the plant to carry out its own amelioration. Chop and drop, and leaving leaves and needles, where this does not impact on other plant growth, is, therefore, a more appropriate management tool.

Chop and drop is the preferred management technique for perennials.

Gardening for Carbon Sequestration

The vital role of soils in the sequestration of carbon was considered earlier in this chapter. The recent re-evaluation of the potential of soils to offer highly effective carbon sequestration opens up the concept of carbon management being considered as a crop, or primary goal in garden management. The humic compounds that build soil structure and hold on to plant nutrients to prevent them leaching through the soil, contain 60 per cent carbon. This vital ecosystem service provided by soil, carbon storage, should, therefore, inform management decisions; for example, the burning of leaves and garden waste as a method of disposal, which releases carbon and other pollutants, should be replaced with deep mulching or composting to sequester a proportion of the carbon they contain.

Many governments around the world have ambitious tree-planting programmes that are aimed at net zero targets. The role of the humus-rich soils that forms under such tree plantings allows for very considerable carbon sequestration to take place over the life of the new planting. This carbon sequestration by soil, while often omitted from calculations. is of vital importance.

This concept is of huge importance when calculating the net positive impact of gardens, with soil carbon sequestration being able to offset some of the more problematic aspects of garden management.

Farming Microorganisms

Plants farm microorganisms. They do this in a zone called the rhizosphere (*rhiza* means root in Greek). This is the area where the plant root and the soil interface with each other. There are three distinct zones within the rhizosphere: the endorhizosphere, where microorganisms live within gaps, crevices and the free spaces between plant cells; the rhizoplane is the area immediately adjacent to the root; while the ectorhizosphere extends the zone to the rest of the soil. Within this zone, the plant provides essential microbes with a habitat that is enriched with decaying cells shed by the root, along with an exudate or mucilage, which eases the roots' movement through the soil. This mucilage is also a source of nutrition to the bacteria and other microorganisms. In return, these farmed organisms further break down organic matter in a process known as mineralisation. This vital process releases soluble inorganic compounds, which the adjacent root hairs are able to absorb. In simple terms, the plant provides food and habitat for the bacteria, which in turn provide essential elements, such as nitrogen, magnesium and potassium, to the plant.

Within the rhizosphere, fungi also a play a role. They assist the plant with the uptake of water. They also help the root to absorb essential elements, such as phosphorus. These fungi, which are specific to different plant species, form a special, mutually beneficial relationship with the plant. The plant benefits, as the fungal hyphae are able to access the microscopic pores within the soil and extract water that is otherwise unavailable to the plant. The huge network of fungal hyphae also greatly increases the area of the root, enhancing nutrient absorption. The fungi freely pass the water and the essential elements into the plant root. In exchange the plant root allows the fungal hyphae access to stored sugars. This symbiotic relationship between plant roots and specific fungal species is called mycorrhizal.

Mycorrhizal relationships are rarer within cultivated gardens but are widespread in nature. Indeed, it has been suggested that many trees and other plant species rely on this relationship for their very survival. As do the fungi.

Rethinking Soil Management

As we develop an understanding of the unseen ecosystem that exists within the soil, it is natural that our approach to soil management will also develop and change.

Soil management will no longer centre around primary cultivations such as digging; but around concepts such as carbon sequestration, allowing plant roots to form associations with fungal hyphae, along with practices that building up strong soil structure, which will enable our soils to become more climate resilient.

The toolkit developed in Chapter 1 allows us to develop these new strategies and management practices:

- Rethink.
- Reduce and reuse.
- Regenerate.
- Record, Reflect, Repeat.

One of the key concepts of sustainable gardening is minimal, or reduced, interventions. This concept requires rethinking to take place to determine which interventions are vital to plant health. While one may be adopting minimal cultivation practices, it may prove necessary to, for example, dig out perennial weed from an area where it is inappropriate. Planned interventions should be designed to boost microbial actions, enhance the creation of crumbs, enhance mycorrhizal relationships and ensure that the soil is sequestrating the maximum carbon possible to combat climate change.

As the practice of digging has a negative impact on macro- and microorganisms, brings weed seeds to the surface, disrupts mycorrhizal relationships, breaks down and weakens soil crumbs and releases carbon from the soil, it can be argued that it is a technique that is best avoided. This concept can be developed to limit all soil disturbance, as hoeing, for example, has a similar (but lesser) negative impact on soil. Deep mulching can be used to replace the hoe, with occasional interventions that disturb the soil carried out only if necessary. Digging should be eliminated or reduced as much as is practicable. There will be situations where digging or soil disturbance is essential, for example the removal of root crops in productive areas or the removal of failed plants in other areas of the garden. However, the practice of digging as fundamental cultivation activity has no place within a sustainable garden.

Chapter 9 will further consider the concept of minimal cultivation or no-dig gardening as a management tool.

Soil bacteria are essential for the mineralisation of organic matter but can be negatively impacted by nutrient salts. These nutrient salts are often applied to our gardens though the use of natural or synthetic fertilizers, or through the use of animal manures. The fertilizer salts reduce the bacterial populations, which in turn reduce the mineralisation of organic matter. This is masked by the free availability of nutrient salts, which encourage excessive plant growth. This plant growth then requires staking or is particularly prone to pests and diseases. Once the fertilizer salts have leached through the soil, or been taken up by the plant, the bacterial population can be so reduced that it is no longer effective in mineralisation to meet the needs of the plant, and so a further application of fertilizer is required, leading to a downward spiral that is hugely damaging to the soil ecosystem. The fertilizer nutrients leached through the soil can enter watercourses, leading to eutrophication, which causes algal blooms, can create dead zones and can kill fish. It is worth noting that these same nutrient salts are present in animal manures, and so these should be used in small quantities or avoided.

Composted green waste contains very low concentrations of these mineral salts, and so can be applied to the soil, often as a deep mulch, to allow soil macroorganisms to move it into the soil profile, prior to decomposition and mineralisation by soil microorganisms.

Rethinking the way we garden to promote soil health is not limited to reduced cultivation and reduced fertilizer inputs. The reduction of other chemical interventions within the garden should be considered. Fungicides, for example, are widely used to control a range of plant diseases from black spot on roses to mildew on clematis. These fungicides wash into the soil, interrupting and interfering with mycorrhizal relationships, to the detriment of plant health and growth.

Soil-Management Plans

Soil-management plans are excellent tools to encourage active reflection on the potential impacts of interventions.

Soil-management plans offer a number of significant benefits, including:

- The improvement of soil health.
- Benefits to plant growth.
- Protection of the soil.
- Enhanced carbon sequestration.
- Reduced spend.
- Boosting biodiversity.

Soil-management plans originated in farming and were originally devised to help farmers to develop their soil. Farm-based, soil-management plans are typically more detailed and technically demanding to produce than the version being proposed here. (The UK Government website has more information on this aspect of soil-management planning.)

Within a garden setting, soil-management plans can be simple and straightforward documents to encourage thought and to inform how we are going to

The Problem with Fertilizers

Some controlled-release fertilizers are bound in a resin coat, which persists in the soil.

As gardeners we need to rethink our relationship with fertilizers.

While there is a case for continuing the use of fertilizers in container gardening, where plants are grown in a sustainably sourced growing medium, or in productive growing, plants grown in the soil should, as far as is practicable, be grown without the use of synthetic fertilizers.

- Synthetic fertilizers produce soft growth, which, as we will see in Chapter 5, is prone to attack from pests and pathogens.
- Synthetic fertilizers' manufacture leads to significant carbon emissions in manufacture and transport.
- All fertilizers disrupt the natural systems plants use to gain nutrition from the soil, they disrupt mycorrhizal relationships and have a negative effect on soil bacteria. This means that, once the nutrient salts provided have been leached out of the soil, or taken up by the plant, the natural mechanisms that the plant was relying on are no longer in place and so the plant is dependent on further applications of fertilizer.
- Some controlled-release fertilizers are bound in a resin coat, which persists in the soil.

Many gardeners may argue that they have specific plants that require regular applications of fertilizer. If these are not applied, then significant deficiency symptoms manifest. It could be argued that the principle of right plant, right place should be applied, and replacement plant species should be selected that do not require such potentially damaging inputs. It is, however, fully accepted that such plants may be central to the garden design, be of significance or have sentimental value, in which case the concept that gardens should be considered as a whole to be net positive, can be applied to allow for their continued cultivation.

work with natural processes to enhance the status of the soils under our care.

The planning process involves a series of different steps. The table (overleaf) is intended as a useful starting point when developing a garden soil-management plan.

This table, when complete, can be considered as both a benchmark and as a plan to inform all soil-management decisions. It should be reviewed on a regular (minimum annual) basis. It should detail how soil is managed at present, and identify issues or problems associated with the soil, both from a sustainability and practical basis. The final column allows us to consider the actions that can be taken to help natural processes to resolve the identified problems.

It may become apparent that separate tables may be required for grassed areas, productive areas and plantings or woodland gardens, as each of these areas requires different management interventions. For

Developing a garden soil-management plan

Criteria/area for consideration	Soil status at present	Identified problems	Appropriate actions
How is the soil currently managed? i.e. dug over in the autumn			
What type of soil is it, i.e. what texture is the soil, sandy, silt, clay?			
Is the garden close to watercourses or wildlife habitats?			
Are there existing soil problems, e.g. compaction?			
Are there earthworms visible in the soil when cultivated?			
What is the soil pH?			

example, the productive garden may currently be dug over annually, the borders may be forked and mulch applied over in the winter/early spring, and the grassed areas may be spiked to improve aeration annually.

The next step is to consider if the soil in these areas exhibits issues. Is it droughty? Does it crack in the summer sun? Does it set hard? Does water pool on the surface during the winter? Is it hard to dig?

The final column considers the actions that can be taken to enhance natural processes that can remedy these issues. These actions can include: the replacement of plants exhibiting poor growth with plant species that favour the soil conditions on site; replacing digging or forking with applications of deep organic mulches; transitioning to minimal cultivation techniques; or eliminating spring fertilizer applications.

The next area for consideration is to identify the type of soil we have. The most accurate way to determine this is to send samples of soil to a laboratory for analysis based on the proportions of the different sized rock particles present in the soil. However, there are many flow charts available online that can take us through the process of adding water to a soil sample and then assessing the texture manually to ascertain if it is gritty (sandy soil), soapy (silt soil) or sticky (clay soil).

Once we have an understanding of the soil type, for example a silty loam, we can then investigate the characteristics of such a soil. Sandy soils tend to hold less water, they are earlier to warm in the spring and faster to cool in the autumn, and they do not hold on to plant nutrients well. While clay soils tend to hold more water, they are, therefore, slower to warm in the spring and

later to cool in the autumn, and hold on to plant nutrients strongly due to a process called cation exchange capacity.

We cannot change the textural class of the soil and, from a sustainable perspective, this would be inappropriate. Each type of soil offers a unique set of advantages and limitations. Sustainable gardening practices would amend the palette of plants to suit the soil condition, rather than amend the soil conditions to suit the plants.

The proximity of the garden to watercourses and wildlife habitats should be considered. Close proximity requires careful management to ensure that there is no run-off from our gardens or the leaching of plant nutrients.

Another aspect for consideration is whether there are any identified soil problems. These could include a grey mottling in clay referred to as gleying, or hard pans or impenetrable layers within the soil. While many books have been written on soil drainage to rectify gleying, these tend to only be appropriate on larger areas, such as sports turf. The drainage of land is also inconsistent with sustainable gardening, which involves looking for the opportunities that the site offers with minimal amelioration. Low-lying areas, prone to flooding in the winter, which have gleyed soil profiles can be considered as ideal locations for constructing rain gardens or swales, which can be filled with species that favour such conditions. Pans and hard layers in the soil are more problematic. These can be caused by repeated rotavating to the same level, or even repeated digging to the same level. Minimal cultivation practices will prevent such problems from occurring. However, it is acknowledged that it may be necessary to deep cultivate to break up such layers, before leaving soil organisms to do the job of maintenance.

A useful tool in measuring soil health is a count of the number of worms present within the soil profile. A high worm population suggests a soil rich in organic matter, while a low worm count suggests the opposite. The application of organic matter to the soil as a deep mulch of garden compost will help to boost worm population in most non-acidic soils.

Measuring the pH of a soil is vital in helping us to understand its characteristics. Samples can be sent to analytical laboratories, or tests can be made with chemical test kits; however, these rarely offer the level of accuracy required. The key criteria with regard to soil pH are to identify it accurately and then ensure that this informs plant selections, rather than try to change it.

A key aspect in developing and enhancing soil-management plans is the recording of issues. This process affords the opportunity to research and consider the most appropriate sustainable practices, to review interventions or simply to amend the palette of plants being cultivated.

Soil-management plans can be incorporated into broader garden health plans, which are considered in more detail in Chapter 5.

CHAPTER 4

PLANTS AND PLANTING

It's surely our responsibility to do everything within our power to create a planet that provides a home not just for us, but for all life on Earth.
David Attenborough

The Right Plant

Many plant producers are striving to produce plants to the highest standards of sustainability. Greenhouses can be heated using carbon-neutral technologies. Peat-, plastic- and pesticide-free production methods can be adopted, water footprints can be reduced. Staff can be paid at, or above, the living wage, with zero-hour contracts being avoided. Local production units minimise transport emissions. The alternative is plants that are produced in glasshouses heated by fossil fuels, growing in peat-based growing media, by staff who are on zero-hour contracts or paid at the minimum wage. Transport of plants from Europe or further afield adds to the carbon footprint of these plants, along with associated biosecurity risks.

Procurement decisions are vitally important in supporting those producers who are on a sustainability journey. These procurement decisions could also take into account the potential of the development of a small nursery area within a garden. Swedish horticulturist Peter Korn advocates growing our own plants in sand beds. These should be constructed to have 200mm (8in) depth of horticultural sand. Seeds can be sown into such beds to produce seedlings with strong root systems. Cuttings can also be rooted in these beds and divisions planted out, to produce plants for planting the following year.

Case Study: The Temperate House

Harry Watkins, Director at St Andrew's Botanic Garden, as part of their sustainability journey, has turned off the heat to their temperate glasshouse, which in one move has significantly reduced the garden's carbon footprint. The argument put forward is that in a climate emergency the only justification for burning fossil fuels to heat a glasshouse would be education or science.

The temperate house decommissioned and deglazed is in the process of being repurposed as a pergola structure for climbing plants hardy to Fife in Scotland.

If, for reasons of available space, time, skill or set-up costs, we are unable to grow the plants that we require for our garden, then it is important to develop procurement strategies that favour those who have high sustainability and biosecurity standards.

Six Key Considerations When Sourcing Plant Material

1. Are the Plants Locally Produced?

The first part of this process is to define the term local. The location of the garden will, to a considerable extent, define the term. A garden within the M25 may have a different definition of local to one that is based in the Highlands of Scotland. It is important to also note that some horticultural definitions of local suggest young plants imported from Europe can be considered to be locally grown if they spend a period in excess of twelve weeks on the nursery. Many plant producers buy in young plug plants, often from European suppliers. These are grown on and sold as locally grown plants. While the ideal definition of local is a plant propagated and grown on a nursery within a given radius of the garden, it is up to the person engaged in procurement to define this very important term for their garden. Biosecurity, carbon emissions from transportation and the creation of strong, local economies are the critical sustainability factors that drive this consideration.

2. Where Does the Supplier Stand on Plastics?

Plant production can involve high uses of plastic or it can be virtually free of plastic usage. Plant producers traditionally grow plants from seed or cuttings, which are inserted into plastic module trays. The resulting plants are potted into plastic liners, (7cm/3in plastic pots) and then potted on to 1 or 2ltr plastic pots. A plastic label is often inserted at this stage. The pots are then inserted into plastic trays as part of the dispatch process, holding the plants in place on the Danish trolleys that are widely used in the industry. Critical factors to consider when sourcing plants with a minimum

Plants produced in peat-free compost within the garden using recycled pots and trays can reduce the garden's carbon footprint.

plastic footprint include ascertaining if the plant producer audits their plastic use. Is there a small team of people reviewing alternative materials? Are alternatives trialled? Are the results of these trials used to inform changes to the production process? Is the plant producer committed to working towards a plastic-free future? Other checks can include ascertaining if module trays and liners are washed for reuse. Is plastic waste recycled or sent to landfill? Are recycled plastics used? Are plastics used recyclable?

Some plastics are highly recyclable, and many plant producers have moved towards using polyethylene terephthalate (PET) based plastics. These are more commonly associated with plastic drinks' bottles. This plastic is highly recyclable, although the recycling process uses energy, which comes from power stations that often burn fossil fuels. For horticultural use, which is often the production of short-lived plants for summer displays (bedding plants), the PET plastic has a

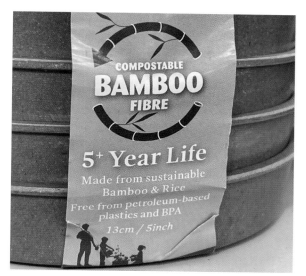

Bamboo and rice fibre pots and saucers are removing plastics from plant production.

Plastic pots, with plastic labels on plastic trays – gardening is sometimes far from green.

A crop of single-use plastic labels, promoting plant sales, but at a huge environmental cost.

UV light inhibitor added to allow plant roots to grow to the edge of containers. It is also worth noting that while these containers are collected for recycling by 94 per cent of councils in the UK, the plastic should be washed free of all growing media and plant debris, as contaminated plastics are problematic from a recycling perspective.

A more sustainable procurement strategy may be to specify bare-root plants. These plants are generally field grown and lifted and dispatched when dormant. Field grown, bare-root plants, often have considerably lower plastic, water and carbon footprints.

When specifying plants, smaller is better. Smaller plants, even when pot grown, offer reduced plastic, water and carbon footprints.

The auditing of a supplier with regard to their plastic footprint also includes the dispatch and delivery process, especially if this is mail order. Are the plants packed and shipped in sustainable and recyclable materials, for example shredded cardboard, newspaper and wood straw, the boxes secured with paper, rather than plastic tape.

When auditing plastic use, check deliveries for bubble wrap, plastic foam and adhesive plastic tape.

Paper tapes offer a more sustainable solution.

3. What is Your Water Footprint?

Water footprinting is a relatively new concept. Chapter 11 explores in greater detail the issues around water usage. Mains water is often scarce during periods of drought, river extraction impacts on wildlife downstream, borehole water cannot be considered to be sustainable, as it is often not replaceable, and can be considered to be fossil water, and even the water captured from the roofs of buildings is problematic as this process of capture removes the water from the natural environment.

Procurement questions relate to the source of water that is used on the nursery. Are strategies in place to reduce water usage? Is water captured and recirculated to reduce the water footprint? Is there a strategy and a desire on the part of the nursery to monitor and work on strategies to reduce their water usage?

4. What is the Carbon Footprint of the Nursery?

The carbon footprint of the nursery is based on numerous factors; for example, the average distance staff commute to work, the source of heat that is used with the glasshouses, whether the electrical supply is based on green or renewable tariffs. Some plant producers are significantly reducing their carbon footprint. Measures used include the promotion of low-carbon commuting, such as through cycle to work schemes that offer discounted bicycles and other benefits. Some companies are offering schemes to help toward the purchase/rental of local housing, to reduce emissions

Sustainable gardeners, you have been warned – do not lean your bikes against fast growing plants!

from commuting. Others are installing air source heat pumps, with small solar electricity generation to provide the power required to run the heat pumps. Others are investing in electric delivery vehicles.

Key questions involve ascertaining if the supplier is auditing and measuring their carbon footprint. Do they have carbon-reduction plans, and are these being implemented?

Plant specification practices that reduce the carbon footprint include timing of plantings to avoid the need for plant material to be forced, the specification of smaller plant material and waiting until there is a delivery run scheduled for your area.

5. Are the Plant-Production Systems Sustainable?

Are plant suppliers using production technologies that support sustainability? Has the production process been audited to ensure measurable improvements are being made? The key areas of concern are the sourcing of growing media. Local sourcing reduces the emissions caused by transport. The avoidance of peat usage is another significant area. The Wildlife Trusts estimate that peatlands store 8,000 tonnes of carbon per hectare. Other areas for investigation include the usage of synthetic fertilizers, along with the usage of pesticides and fungicides, which can cause lower establishment rates due to their deleterious effects on mycorrhizal relationships and the use of herbicides.

6. Is Everyone in the Supply Chain Treated Fairly?

Does the plant producer foster a safe, secure and inclusive workplace? Are staff safe? Do all staff have secure contracts of employment? Are staff appreciated and fairly rewarded for their work? Is there cultural diversity in the workforce that is reflective of the demography of the area? Does the plant producer audit its full supply chain to ensure that all those engaged experience similar employment experiences? These checks may involve regular audits of the supply chain to ensure compliance with the Modern Slavery Act (2015) or that all employees of those in the supply chain are paid the living wage.

Models of excellence include suppliers who provide multilingual signage, respect cultures and traditions, supply prayer rooms and support flexible working practices.

The white card contains whitefly scales, which have been parasitised by the chalcid wasp *Encarsia formosa*. These cards are hung on crop plants. Adult *Encarsia formosa* emerge from the scales and parasitise whitefly found within the glasshouse.

The Right Place

The sourcing of sustainably produced plants is half of the planting equation. Specifying the right plant for the right place balances this process. The specification process involves taking into account a wide and sometimes conflicting range of information. First there is the overall look of the area. Does the design intend this to be a formal or informal area? Are there historical contexts that will apply filters to our plant-selection process? Having ascertained these basics, the next layer of information can be considered. The findings of the site analysis, discussed earlier in this book, can be applied. The final filters are applying how a changing climate may impact on the palette of plants available to us. This final filter is the most problematic, and many different groups and organisations are working on this, including the Trees and Design Action group (TDAG), who are linking environmental stresses to tree physiology and morphology.

Dr Ross Cameron, a senior lecturer at the University of Sheffield, is a specialist in climate change, who has been working on the topic of how a changing climate impacts on planting decisions.

Key findings with regard to the impacts of a changing climate include:

- Average temperatures have risen by 1°C since 1900.
- Average temperatures are predicted to rise by 2.4–4.1°C by 2046.
- Higher temperatures, along with higher levels of light and CO_2 will boost plant growth.
- More challenging weather conditions may negatively impact on plant growth.
- By 2050, our climate will resemble those of places that are 1,000km (620 miles) south.
- By 2050, our eastern climate may be drier and our western climate wetter.
- There will be greater frequency of extreme weather events, such as many weeks of average rainfall being recorded in one large rainfall event.

These scientific predictions can be further evaluated to consider the impacts that they may have on plant selection:

- Resilience to wetting and drying cycles is predicted to be of greater significance. This impact is likely to be more profound on lighter soils, with lower water-holding capabilities. Plants cool themselves through the evaporation of water from their leaves and so, when water is in short supply, this increases environmental stress on the plant. Plant specifiers could respond to this information by investigating the ranges of plants that grow in areas that already experience these conditions. Current areas of interest include the steppe, others suggest looking at dry riverbeds, which flood in winter and dry in the late spring/summer. It is predicted that plant breeders will be considering these factors and breeding plants that are better able to cope with these conditions. It is also anticipated that leading gardens will trial new plant introductions to identify their resilience to these new and harsher conditions.
- There is some evidence emerging from research work undertaken at the University of Sheffield that wet soil conditions in summer have a greater impact on plant survival than wet soils during periods of inactivity, such as winter. There is also evidence that naturally occurring plant forms are more resilient than plants that have been bred to be more floriferous. The plant-breeding process referred to in the preceding point should, therefore, be based on naturally occurring forms, rather than those previously selected for larger flowers or more floriferous habits.
- Plant-selection strategies in the future are likely to be based on an increasing understanding of the principle of ecophysiology, which is the study of how biotic and abiotic factors interact with the physiology of an organism.
- The concept of native plants will require careful review. The term is currently problematic as there is no definition or general agreement over how long a plant has had to live within a geographical area to be considered native. It is unlikely that the plant was native to the region during the last ice age and, therefore, it is fair to pose the question, how long does a species have to grow in a location for it to be considered to be native? As the climate changes, a native plant suited to one climate may be unsuited to one from 1,000km (620 miles) south. Horticulturists are now considering the concept of near natives to describe the plants that may be able to adapt to a changing climate.

- Provenance is becoming an ever more important factor when selecting seed and plant material. This concept suggests that the same plant species that is acclimatised to growing in, for example, Barcelona, is more likely to be able to adapt to a changing climate than one acclimatised to living in northern Scotland. The concept of provenance is particularly interesting as it could allow the continued cultivation of plant species that are part of existing ecosystems, rather than require the introduction of new, more novel species. However, these may have a role to play as well. The Forestry Commission, responding to climate change, suggest that rather than simply specifying natives for woodland planting schemes, consideration should be given to increasing the genetic diversity within plantings to add a further layer of resilience.
- The concept of genetic diversity is also being applied to ornamental plantings. The key concept in this situation is that the specification of named varieties and cultivars limits genetic diversity and so site conditions that may impact on one cultivar would impact the whole planting. The use of seed, rather than cutting-raised perennials, shrubs and trees, potentially offers a much wider genetic diversity and so more resilient plantings that may be able to cope better with changing climates.
- There is a school of thought that suggests that the impact of the surroundings can have as wide an impact on plant growth and survival as genetic diversity. Trees grown as individual specimens within hard-landscaped areas, even when planted to the most appropriate specifications, rarely outgrow or outperform those growing in more ecological settings, such as grown as groups or within plant communities in more natural environments, for example in grassland. This has been observed with tree plantings 5m (16ft) apart, with the restricted growth of species planted within paving compared with those in grassland.

Gardens are filled with diversity. There are 50,000 types of food plant in the world. The Kew Gardens' database lists 32,500 different herbs. Significantly, the RHS have reported that their online 'my garden tool'

What are Abiotic and Biotic Factors?

Many environmental factors impact on plant growth, from prevailing winds and frost to pests and diseases. These factors can be classified as being either biotic or abiotic.

Biotic factors include the organic matter within the soil and the impact of other living things, for example competition from spontaneous plants for water and light, or reduction in photosynthetic area of a leaf from pest attack.

Abiotic factors include wider environmental factors, such as temperature, intensity of sunlight, wind, rain and frost.

A changing climate poses biotic risks, such as the presence of new plant health risks.

A changing climate poses abiotic risks, such as the impact of high winds, periods of waterlogging and periods of drought.

has recorded the cultivation of 77,000 different types of plant, recorded by 117,000 gardeners. This diversity of plant material will be vital, as the climate changes and favours some plant species over others.

The Right Purpose

The concept of right plant, right place can be extended to include, for the right purpose. Plants perform a wide range of purposes. These purposes can include vertical and horizontal screening, the production of food for humans and for wildlife, the promotion of well-being and the positive impacts that plants can have on mental health.

While considering the selection of species for planting, it is important to ensure that the plants specified are selected to perform specific purposes.

Grasses can be cultivated to provide form and movement within a scheme, but with the primary purpose of providing a home-grown chopped mulch for use in the garden. Other plants might be specified to provide plant-support structures for annuals, herbaceous perennials and for use in productive growing settings.

Sedums and other species can be specified to create green roofs, which create habitats and slow the flow of water during periods of high rainfall. Similarly, plants can be specified to filter and slow the movement of water, for example within swales and rain gardens.

As stated within Chapter 2, plants can be specified to perform a range of ecosystem services: wall shrubs cooling buildings in hot summers, while providing nesting and perching sites for wild birds, they produce food for pollinators and fruit for wild birds and small mammals.

Issues relating to food security are thought to become more significant in a changing climate. It has been predicted that a 2°C increase in temperatures could result in many rice-growing sites to be no longer environmentally appropriate. Against these predicted

scenarios it may be prudent to consider the specification of edible plants within general planting schemes. The production of food not only creates more resilience from a food-security perspective, it also has a significant and positive impact on mental health and wellness benefits. Edible landscapes and productive growing can also be important tools to raise people out of food poverty.

The specification of plants to provide cover to the soil surface over winter periods to deflect rain and preserve the developing crumb structures was discussed in Chapter 3. The importance of the roots of such cover crops in stabilising soil and reducing the incidence of erosion is also likely to become more significant.

Developing a Garden-Based Resilience Database

The specification of the right plant, for the right place, to perform the right purpose in a changing climate is a complex and difficult task. Reliable sources of information are rare and can conflict. Even reliable sources of information can suggest that a particular species favours dry conditions, while another suggests planting on riverbanks near to bodies of flowing water.

Within gardens there can be significant differences in temperature and rainfall, making plant specification an even more complex task. Plant records are maintained by a number of different organisations to manage their living collections. These records record key plant information, from name and family, to the date of planting and the results of annual health inspections. Most importantly, these systems also record plant deaths, and allow the inclusion of reason codes or free text entry to record cause of death. These systems allow for the development of data that can be used to inform plant selection and specification. A simple system can *be* created in a spreadsheet (*see* the table opposite).

The data captured by formally recording factors as basic as plant deaths to identify a range of species that do not perform well within the garden is a vital management tool.

Purpose lists can also be created to drive plant specifications.

Green roofs increase biodiversity in gardens; they also slow down water discharge, helping to reduce the risk of flooding.

Construction detail of a green roof installed at RHS Garden Wisley.

An example plant record

Accession number	Genus	Species	Cultivar	Year planted	Health status	Notes

Example Purpose Lists

Example 1

Purpose	Production of plant-support structures for the productive garden Production of wigwam structures to support sweet peas
Suitable plants	*Corylus avellana* (hazel)
Notes	Grow in groups of three or five Coppice once every two years Can produce nuts Can produce cover Perfect underplanted with *Primula vulgaris*
Soil type	Alkaline/neutral soil

Example 2

Purpose	To produce mulch for the garden
Suitable plants	*Miscanthus* spp.
Notes	Range of colours available Can look good when planted with *Verbena bonariensis* 'Ferner Osten' is a large form that can be used to produce mulch. 'Starlight' is more suited to smaller spaces.
Soil type	Wide range of pH tolerated

Example 3

Purpose	To attract orange tip butterflies
Suitable plants	*Cardamine pratensis*
Notes	Pale pink flowers in April Eggs are laid on the flower stalks Caterpillars eat the leaves, pupate and emerge as orange tip butterflies Note: It is the male that has the orange-tipped wings
Soil type	Damp soils, in hollows

Planting Techniques

The timing of planting operations is critical to ensure that inputs are minimised. Spring planting was favourable when there were reliable spring rains. Recently, there has been very low rainfall in the spring period and so autumn planting is now favoured to reduce the need to irrigate freshly planted areas. Late autumn is also an ideal time to plant as it ensures that plants will not have required forcing, bare-root plants can be specified and soil conditions are still warm to encourage root development prior to winter.

A number of leading gardens have reviewed the process of planting, to ensure this has the minimum negative environmental impact. Planting with minimal disturbance to the soil is a key criterion and a significant change to traditional techniques. Soil disturbance, which is sometimes a necessary part of cultivation, should be minimised where practicable. As well as being time-consuming it releases greenhouse gases such as CO_2 and NO_2.

The ten steps to planting sustainably are:

1. Prepare the plant for planting; if pot grown, the growing media should be gently removed until the flare (the top of the root system) is seen.
2. A planting hole should be excavated to match the depth and width of the root system.
3. The soil at the base and sides of the hole should be left undisturbed.
4. No organic matter should be added.
5. No fertilizer should be added.
6. The plant should be placed in the hole, and positioned with the surface of the growing media/rootball 2—3mm above the soil surface.
7. The gaps between the side of the root ball and the soil should be filled in.
8. The soil should be firmed gently.
9. The plant should be watered-in using rainwater harvested on site. If additional watering is needed, place a leaky bucket adjacent to the plant.
10. Apply a mulch of 70mm (3in) depth, ensuring this does not come in contact with the trunk of the plant.

Some of these steps may seem counter-intuitive to those who trained in horticulture some time ago. Plants are often potted by machine, and often have their flare low in the pot. If this is not corrected at

planting, it can lead to the lifting of bark, the rotting of the stem and plant failure. The limited size of the planting hole serves two purposes. It limits the release of greenhouse gasses from the soil, but it also prevents disturbed soil settling, which results in the root ball sinking, and the plant being planted too deeply. This is also the rationale behind eliminating the addition of organic material, as the decomposition results in the root ball sinking. Fertilizer is also eliminated to encourage the plant to send foraging roots into the soil. Providing a source of fertilizer close to the plant prevents the roots developing a relationship with soil bacteria, which are killed by fertilizer salts, reduces the chance of the plant establishing mycorrhizal relationships and discourages the formation of foraging roots.

Plant Establishment

Post planting, if the right plant has been chosen for the prevailing site conditions, then no further watering should be required. (As with all new plantings, it may appear as if the plant is not establishing as there is little extension growth. This is normal as most growth will be occurring below soil level with the establishment of a root system.) Spontaneous plants, such as weeds, should be minimal as the mulch will reduce the incidence of annual weed growth. Perennial weeds will need careful removal, if appropriate; it is recognised that this may require soil disturbance.

Six tips for effective plant establishment:

1. Learn to read the plant. It is important to be able to identify initial signs of stress in the plant. Signs of stress vary from species to species but can include changes to the texture of the leaf. Leaf colour can appear duller. The leaves of some plant species roll slightly when under water stress. A useful tool to investigate these stress responses is to observe a *Chlorophytum comosum* (spider plant) When this plant is under severe water stress, the leaves dull and they fold to reduce water loss.
2. If irrigation is necessary, despite an accurate assessment of site and appropriate plant selection, then a tree watering bag can be used. This bag is zipped into position around the trunk of the tree and the bag is then filled with water, which leaks

slowly into the surface of the soil. An old, leaky bucket can also be used for this purpose.

3. Give the plant time to establish. There is an old adage that relates to plant establishment: *in the first year they sleep, in the second year they creep and in the third year they leap.* In the first year or two, the plant is producing an extensive root system; this is to anchor the plant in the ground, but also to forage for nutrients and water. During this time, it can be tempting to move the plant to what is deemed a more favourable position; however, this will only result in stress to the plant and delay establishment.

4. Avoid mycorrhizal treatments. In Chapter 3, the importance of mycorrhizal relationships was introduced. These relationships are between individual fungal species and individual plant roots. Different plant species form relationships with different fungal species. This process is more advantageous when it occurs naturally. A sachet of general-purpose mycorrhizal fungi may be effective; however, there is evidence that the impact of introduced fungal species to the soil may be that other fungal species are out-competed, allowing the introduced species to dominate and so restrict the formation of relationships with more appropriate fungal species. A low-cost, sustainable strategy may be to use the traditional technique of when, for example, planting a beech hedge, to mix some soil from under an existing, healthy beech hedge into the planting soil being used to infill around the root ball, thus naturally inoculating the plant with beneficial fungi appropriate to the species.

5. As the planting establishes and matures, it may be that errors appear. While the intent may be to create plantings of different heights, that flower at different times, planted at densities to shade out spontaneous plants, errors can occur. Plant failure can impact the planting; low-growing plants can grow behind taller ones. Some species may spread to the point of becoming invasive and threaten the survival of other plants. Best practice in these situations is to record the issues by taking photographs. Add these to the records being kept. Then carry out remedial actions, which can include removal of dead and invasive species, pruning or replacement planting, at the appropriate time.

6. Record all the key data in a spreadsheet. The version suggested earlier in this chapter could

be developed to include the name of plant suppliers to allow the tracking of quality of plants supplied based on percentage survival rates after two years.

Retraining Our Eyes

In my own garden, I have for many years battled celandine. It has, despite my best efforts, spread along one entire side of the garden. However, when applying the toolkit developed in the introduction, rethinking has revealed that it is in fact causing no harm; it is low-growing and disappears as quickly as it grows up. The flowers are important sources of nectar for emerging queen bumblebees and other insects. The newly named celandine borders are becoming fuller with these spontaneous plants, with a corresponding increase in bumblebee nests in the garden.

Irrigation bags can be zipped around the trunks of newly planted trees. They weep water into the soil to aid establishment.

Case Study: Peter Korn's Swedish Garden

Swedish plantsman and designer, Peter Korn.

Peter Korn's garden at Klinta Trädgård near Malmö. Planting is based around the concept of microhabitats, with plantings based around the ecological niche of the plants.

Peter Korn is a Swedish plantsman and designer. Korn's book, *Giving Plants What They Want*, introduced a radically different approach to gardening. Korn's approach to gardening is based on the observation of plant species growing in the wild. 'Try to work out what grows to the south, and the north. Take note what the plants look like', explains Korn. 'The plants we buy, grown in a perfect, moist growing media, with plentiful nutrition are not at all like their hardier and more resilient cousins growing on a mountainside in thin soil. Many people buy a plant and then go and find a place for it, without thinking about the plant. Instead think about the plant, what does it want, where does it grow in the wild, where would it choose to grow in the garden.'

Korn's plant-centred approach does not end there. When buying plants, the first process of planting is to wash all growing media from the roots. The plant is then either potted into sand or planted into sand in the garden. The sand is specified to a 0—8mm grade, which is common in Sweden. Establishment of the plants is slower, as they grow large and extensive root systems before developing leaves and flowers. The growing media is washed off the plant to ensure that there are no nutrient salts present, which would inhibit the development of mycorrhizal relationships, which develop strongly in the sand. One of the reasons why the plants grown in the free-draining sand are so resilient to drought, is the fungal hyphae, which are able to extract water and nutrients from the sand, passing these to the plant. 'When you grow without compost you get an ecosystem. However, as is the case with a meadow, but one application of fertilizer and you spoil it for 50 years.' The plants grown using this system are hardier, they are not affected by drought, there is a reduction in the incidence of pest and disease, and Korn adds, 'if they need staking then you know you have done something wrong'.

Plants are propagated directly into sand beds, with cuttings struck directly into the sand. The resulting plants are then lifted and planted out (with large root systems) as required. These root systems support the plants and, even in periods of drought, the garden continues to perform.

With regard to the selection of plant species, the key principle is to look for plants that come from areas with a more extreme climate than the garden they will be living in. For Sweden, the ideal region is the steppe; plants from this region are resistant to cold, heat and drought.

Natives tend to be avoided as, with a changing climate, 'we no longer have the native climate that they are adapted to'.

Korn argues that when one groups plants from a geographic location, they tend to work together from an aesthetic and from an ecological point of view. Plants that come from a dry meadow will always look good when grown together. Another criterion for plant selection is to consider the root system. Plants with deeper tap roots are more likely to survive in drought conditions, as their roots go deeper. There is also safety in numbers; if one is over-reliant on a particular species and the drought is severe, then the failure is very apparent. Having a mixture of species within a planting spreads the risk. Korn's formula is to choose three star-performing plants for each season, with the other plants being there to support these. The seasonal interest can come from growing plants from slightly different geographical areas.

If the soil is problematic, then the depth of sand is greater; if the soil is good, then the sand is thinner and can almost just be a deep mulch. Once the plants have been planted there is one watering to settle the roots and then there is no further irrigation. The maintenance of the garden is carried out to keep the sand free from organic material. 'Organic matter that is allowed to build up in the sand would encourage weeds and would wick moisture from deep in the sand to the surface where it would evaporate. Without organic matter the sand is dry on top, moisture is trapped deep down where the plant roots and the mycorrhiza are.' Weeds are pulled up and, as we will see in Chapter 6, simply thrown on to the lawn to be mown in; this adds organic matter and nutrition to the lawn. The only other maintenance that the garden receives is a winter burn to remove the dry, dead, top growth before the spring bulbs show through. This aspect is the most problematic from a sustainability perspective as many invertebrate species may be present in the area. A more appropriate technique may be to remove all the material in the late winter/early spring and compost this to use as a mulch in productive growing areas.

Summing up the approach Korn stresses: 'I add no water. In the wild the plants rely only on the rain, no feeds are added or required, as the mycorrhiza take care of that. No compost is added as this is not added in the wild. This way is not strange, this is the way nature gardens, it is traditional gardening that is strange.'

Nine Plants to Try in your Sustainable Garden

Clematis elodi ('Evipo115') (Tudor Patio Series). A compact (50cm), deciduous, shrub-like clematis.

Sedum takesimense Atlantis ('Nonsitnal'). A variegated stonecrop that is drought-tolerant and compact.

Eryngium 'Blue Waves'. A cross between *Eryngium bourgatti* and *Eryngium alpinum*. Compact (50cm), does not need staking.

Isotoma axillaris Fizz 'n' Pop Glowing Purple ('Tmlu 1301'). Grown as an annual, 30cm tall, star-shaped flowers to first frost.

Salvia 'Kisses and Wishes'. Upright, 75cm, flowers all summer to late autumn.

Heliopsis helianthoides var. *scabra* 'Summer Nights'. 1.5m tall, with bronzed leaves, flowers from summer to early autumn.

Helenium 'Sahin's Early Flowerer'. 50–90cm tall, flowers summer to autumn.

Caryopteris × *clandonensis* 'Summer Sorbet'[PBR]. 75cm tall, with variegated leaves, flowers late summer to early autumn.

Sarcococca (sweet box). 70cm, flowers in the winter, heavenly scent.

CHAPTER 5

GARDEN HEALTH

Great fleas have little fleas upon their backs to bite 'em,
And little fleas have lesser fleas, and so ad infinitum.

Augustus De Morgan

Integrated Pest Management (IPM)

The management of garden health is often problematic. When a large colony of aphids is spotted on roses, the natural reaction is to reach for a spray bottle. The products in such a bottle can vary enormously: some will contain precisely targeted synthetic chemicals, while some contain natural and more organic products, such as pyrethrum. This active ingredient is permitted as a pesticide on organic gardens and is natural and derived from the flowers of *Chrysanthemum cinerariifolium*. It is, however, more environmentally damaging than many synthetic products, as it is broad spectrum, which means it does not just control the target pest, it also kills beneficial insects.

There has to be a better way than simply reacting to a problem by reaching for a product, however benign it might be. In most other areas, health is managed. It is recognised that there are multiple contributory factors that impact on health. The impacts of these factors are identified, monitored and managed.

The horticultural equivalent of this process is Integrated Pest Management (IPM). This system of pest management (which is also effective in the control of plant diseases) involves a number of steps or interventions. The model advocated within sustainable gardening is based on eight key steps, or processes, which lead from one to the other to develop a management strategy.

1. Scouting to Establish the Early Signs of Pest, Disease, Weed or Plant Health Threats

This process involves the careful and deliberate observation of plants to ensure their health status; it involves being able to identify signs of stress and early signs of pest or disease presence on plants. Once potential risks have been identified, they are researched to ensure accurate identification and to establish the extent to which they are a risk to plant health. This is a fundamental concept. As we seek to build biodiversity, there will be more garden visitors. Some caterpillars may be part of the life cycle of rare and endangered species of moths and butterflies, in which case no action is required. Others may be present in high numbers and decimating a particular plant; for example, the larvae spotted on a leaf of *Polygonatum* × *hybridum* (Solomon's seal) may be a sawfly, which impacts on the aesthetics of the plant.

Scouting offers the advantage of early identification of a low level of organisms on plants. It allows time to identify these organisms. This identification allows research to be undertaken to rate whether these organisms pose a risk to plant health. In the case of the Solomon's seal, the sawfly defoliates the plant but does not usually lead to plant death. A management strategy may be that, if the plant is attacked badly every year by a pest that is specific to it, then it may be better to move it to another part of the garden where it is not so visible. It then becomes part of the food web in the garden supporting biodiversity.

Considering biodiversity allows us to rethink the problem. The sawfly is dependent on the Solomon's seal for its survival, and therefore are we not duty bound to support the sawfly in our biodiverse gardens? The sawfly itself can then become part of the garden food web, providing a food source to many different organisms. The space freed up from moving the Solomon's seal can then be used to grow plants that are less likely to be attacked in the same way.

It can therefore be seen that when scouting it is necessary to be able to identify the organism, to research its full lifecycle, and to fully consider its role in the garden food web. Only when the full role of the organism in the garden food web is fully considered should the possibility of control measures be considered. If it is deemed necessary to control a pest or disease, then the research should turn to an evaluation of the most effective points in the life cycle for effective intervention.

2. Establish a Threshold.

This is a critical stage in the IPM process. At what point can an organism be tolerated and at what point should control measures be implemented? A critical aspect of establishing the threshold for control is asking at what point does the potential harm to the garden ecosystem outweigh the benefits of the organism to the food web. Other aspects of the threshold, especially in productive growing or in the cultivation of flowers for cutting, would be the point at which the value of damage outweighs the

cost of control. Thresholds are, therefore, specific to the organism in question. It would be entirely appropriate for a garden, for example, to take a zero-tolerance policy with regard to cabbage white caterpillars in productive growing areas, while taking no action in the control of leaf-cutter bees that cause damage to the leaves of roses.

It should be remembered at all times that the presence of organisms on plants is simply the sign that our garden is connected with the rest of nature.

3. Control Options 1: Cultural Control

IPM works on the principle that having scouted, identified and determined thresholds, the required actions should be ranked based on their potential negative environmental impacts. The control measures with the least environmental impact are the cultural controls. These could include:

- Quarantine new plant arrivals.
- Only plant healthy stock.
- Ensure that the plant requirements match the site criteria.
- Specify cultivars that are resistant (or partially resistant) to pathogens.
- Rethink: if a plant regularly succumbs to pathogens, is it wise to continue growing it?
- Research: is the plant being cultivated in the best way possible?
- Limit the application of nutrients to reduce the incidence of soft growth, which is susceptible to attack.
- Consider the density of the planting. High planting densities can reduce air movement, creating areas of high humidity that favour fungal pathogens.
- Rethink pruning practices to allow positive air movement through plants.
- Practice crop rotation to reduce the chance of pathogens overwintering and attacking new plantings the following year.
- Alternate hosts could be removed, for example, some weeds can act as alternate hosts for pathogens.
- In protected cultivation, the reduction of temperature can negatively impact on fecundity (the breeding capacity of an organism).

Poor-quality stock can introduce weeds, pests and diseases to the garden. The faded labels indicate old stock, which will be pot-bound. All these plants, including the dead rhubarb, were spotted in a garden centre in August.

- Consider smaller patchwork plantings. There is research to indicate that some invertebrate species only lay eggs when there is a particular volume of host plant present.
- Practice good garden hygiene.
- Dispose of infected plant material appropriately. A hot compost heap breaks down plant material but also kills any eggs or spores. Gardens without this facility should dispose of infected plant material by sending it for off-site hot-composting.
- Predict and anticipate problems, for example, some apps will warn of the potential incidence of blight diseases.
- Irrigation of container-grown plants should be carried out in the morning rather than the evening, to ensure that leaves are not going through the night wet.

4. Control Option 2: Physical Control Methods

Having exhausted the wide range of cultural control methods available, physical control offers the next line of defence. Physical control can be basic, such as the practice of picking slugs off plants as evening falls. It can involve the use of physical barriers such as horticultural fleece, which is often used as a floating mulch to protect carrots from carrot root fly. Other techniques include the use of traps or even the use of a vacuum cleaner to control populations of whitefly in a glasshouse setting. Other physical controls include spraying plants with blasts of water to dislodge pests or netting crops of brassica to protect from cabbage white butterfly or to protect soft fruit from birds.

5. Control Option 3: Biological Controls

If the previous control methods have not proved to be effective, and the pathogen is still posing a risk to plant health, then the next layer of protection is the use of biological control. This concept involves the use of a predator or parasite to control a specific pathogen. An example could be the use of *Bacillus thuringiensis* (a naturally occurring soil bacterium) to control the larval form of the cabbage white butterfly on brassica crops. Other examples of biological control include growing predator strips. These areas are planted with open, nectar-rich flowers, which attract insects such as hoverflies, which lay their eggs on neighbouring plants. The resulting larvae are voracious feeders on aphids.

Cabbage white caterpillars can be hand-picked off plants as a simple, ecological method of pest control.

Cosmos, with its bright and open flowers attracts hoverflies to the garden, who lay eggs amongst aphids, to provide a food source for the resulting larvae.

Hibernacula (piles of twigs and small branches that are left to weather and decay in the garden) provide a habitat for toads and other predators, which control a wide range of garden pests. In a similar way, spider habitats can be created by placing small loops of wire within planted areas, enabling spiders to spin webs and so predate on potential plant pests.

6. Control Option 4: Biostimulants and Deterrents

If the pathogen continues to be problematic, and it is still deemed important to cultivate the plant species, and the threshold for control has been exceeded, then biostimulants or deterrents can be used. Garlic extract is a widely used product that has been demonstrated to protect plants from attack by a wide range of plant pests from slugs to insects. The role of biostimulants to promote growth, along with the role of anti-feedants and deterrents, is an area of considerable research interest at present, as these products could offer an ecologically appropriate method of control.

7. Control Option 5: Chemical Controls

These control measures, which were once first choice and not a last resort option, can be used if all other

A small hibernaculum, created at Sprint Mill Garden in Cumbria.

prevention and control options have proved to be ineffective. Rethinking is required to fully evaluate all of the previous stages to ensure that chemical control is the only option. This includes consideration as to whether the affected plants should be under cultivation. If the decision is made, then research should be undertaken to inform an ecological risk assessment that identifies the potential negative impacts of the manufacture, distribution and impact of the chemical. It should be noted that not all chemical products are the same. There are gradations within chemical controls. There are soap-based products, which dissolve the waxy layer on the target organism thus desiccating it. There are oil-based products, which block spiracles or breathing pores. There are chemicals that have more specific impacts, for example impacting on the nervous system of the pathogen. It is important when considering a chemical control to ensure that it is approved for use in the country where it is being used. For example, many internet sources suggest neem as a suitable product for the control of certain plant pathogens. However, this product is not approved for use in the UK.

Care should be taken with 'folk remedies'. A product should only be used for a purpose with which it has a label recommendation. Washing-up liquid, for example, does not have a label recommendation for use in the control of greenfly on roses, and so is not an approved product. A major limitation in this scenario is that there are no published safe rates of application or dilution, and an assessment has not been made as to how this product impacts on beneficial insects and organisms, or its impact on soil ecology.

8. Evaluation of Results

This final stage in the process allows for the recording, review and reflection of the control measures. Did the interventions have the desired effect? Was the pathogen effectively managed? Were there unexpected side-effects? How could the intervention be improved for use in a future year? The evaluation of the results of intervention should be recorded as part of the overall garden health planning process.

A Wider Perspective

The approach taken by Peter Korn, the Swedish plantsman and designer, was considered in Chapter 4. The approach advocated by Korn, as well as impacting on plants and plantings, also impacts positively on garden health. Korn's garden is almost entirely free of plant pathogens. Korn argues that healthy plants, grown to be tough and hard, are naturally resistant to attack. The mycorrhizal relationships established in the root zone are also documented to provide the plant with a defence against root-borne diseases, in addition to the provision of water and essential elements.

Korn's approach can be classified within IPM strategies as being cultural control, with careful plant selection, the elimination of the feeds that promote soft growth and minimal interventions. Korn travels to the geographical areas to determine the positions favoured by plants in the wild. Is the plant growing in shade cast by rocks? In full sun? Is the ground naturally moisture-retentive and prone to flooding? This concept of looking to the wild to determine plant requirements has been the motivating force behind plant explorations led by botanical gardens and other institutions over many decades.

These wider abiotic impacts on plant growth can be added to the IPM model to develop a model of thinking that is called the Garden Health Plan. This document holistically considers all the risks to plant health posed by a site. It not only identifies abiotic risks, such as frost or wind, but also considers the impacts that these factors can have on plant growth, and how this can influence the plant's responses to pest and pathogen attack. An example could be that plants require the element potassium as part of the secondary thickening process. This process changes soft extension growth to woody growth in many eudicotyledonous plants (a clade of flowering plants, which have two seed leaves on germination). This ripened, woody growth is more able to withstand frost over the winter and so impacts on plant health. Plants with a deficiency of potassium may not develop ripened wood to the same extent as those with a more plentiful supply of potassium. This can lead to frost damage, which reduces photosynthetic area, and so has a wider impact on plant growth.

The Garden Health Plan is a tool that allows the rethinking of plant health risks from the widest biotic and abiotic perspectives. It affords the opportunity to research the way that individual plants respond and adapt to these risks, which allows reflection on both plant selection and cultivation practices. The final stage is to review and reflect on the efficacy of plant selection and cultivation practices. Gardening in a changing climate will introduce new and novel plant health risks. Garden Health Plans offer a management tool to develop holistic plant health strategies that can positively impact on plant health in a sustainable way.

A range of abiotic factors that can impact on plant health, which can be considered when developing a Garden Health Plan, is shown below (it is pertinent to note that these plant health impacts would not be considered within traditional IPM programmes):

- Light levels' impact on plant growth. Insufficient light often leads to weak etiolated growth, while excess light can lead to scorching of leaves.
- Oxygen levels, especially low concentrations of oxygen around the roots of plants (especially during times of active growth), can lead to root death, which can cause wilting of the foliage.
- Temperature. Low temperatures, such as frosts, or high temperatures can negatively impact on plant health. In a changing climate the risk of high-temperature damage is increasing, with most plants exhibiting permanent damage or death at above 46°C. In 2021, a temperature of 54.4°C was recorded in California's Death Valley.
- Water. Periods of drought can negatively impact on plant growth. When water is in short supply, photosynthesis slows or stops. This results in the plant using stored energy in respiration; this energy is, therefore, not available to facilitate growth or for flower initiation and development. Wet soils, especially over the autumn and winter, can increase the prevalence of plant diseases, such as phytophthora. Waterlogged soils reduce the availability of oxygen to plant roots, which in turn can cause root death.
- Wind, in particular salt-laden winds in coastal locations, can impact on plant growth, with storms uprooting trees and constant winds stunting plant growth.

Protect Plant from Frost
Ask a member of staff for more details

When choosing plants for specific locations, one of the considerations is the hardiness of the plant. The RHS publishes a list of hardiness ratings on their website to assist in this process.

The range of abiotic factors that impact on plant growth can be widened to consider plant nutrition. A key consideration is the way that nutrient availability impacts on plant growth and so plant health:

- Phosphorus uptake can be lower in plants that have not developed mycorrhizal relationships. As phosphorus is involved in energy transfer processes in the plant, this can reduce vigour and reduce growth.
- Excessive levels of nitrogen can lead to the promotion of soft growth in shoots and leaves, which can then be prone to attack by a range of pathogens.
- Potassium, when limited, can reduce flowering and fruiting; its impact on secondary thickening, the ripening of wood and cold hardiness has already been considered.
- Soils with a poor, dense structure restrict root growth, and so reduce foraging area for water and nutrients.

These factors interrelate with each other to provide more significant plant health impacts, for example, soils with a poor, dense structure, restrict root growth. In periods of drought, the reduced root system impacts on the ability of the root to take up water. As plant nutrients can only be taken up by the plant in water, the plant has a reduced uptake of nutrients. This may impact on poor growth. There is evidence that plants growing in conditions such as this are unable to move products of photosynthesis and to store these in the roots as starch.

Therefore, leaves have higher levels of sugars within them, making them more attractive to pest attack.

As the different factors that impact on plant health are identified and viewed in a holistic manner, novel interventions can be planned and targeted where they will have the greatest benefit to the plant, while reducing any negative environmental impact. The advanced understanding of how plants interact with planting sites can also be used to determine if the planting decisions are still appropriate. For example, plants growing on sites prone to cold temperatures and frosts could benefit from potassium to increase cold hardiness. A more sustainable option would be to consider the impact of this knowledge on plant selections, and to consider the replacement of these plants with ones that have greater cold hardiness.

A further layer of thinking, which is rarely considered within IPM strategies, is to consider how plant health risks enter the garden:

- Irrigation water can spread diseases such as phytophthora. This is often the case where drainage water is collected in a body of water within the garden, with water being extracted without sterilisation to irrigate garden areas.
- The importation of contaminated growing media or poor storage of growing media can cause pathogens to be introduced.
- The purchase of new plants for planting can introduce new pests and diseases.
- Poor-quality seed can harbour a range of plant health risks, including viral pathogens.

- Wood and bark can import diseases into the garden, including bark- and wood-boring beetles, canker-causing fungi and vascular wilts.
- Pallets that have not been heat-treated to ISPM15 can bring pests into the garden. It is worth noting that significant quantities of plant health risks are transported around the world on pallets. This has led to the requirement for pallets to be stamped to show that they have been kiln-dried or treated chemically. It should be noted that there is evidence that fake pallets are on the increase and so it is not recommended for pallet wood to be used within a garden setting.
- Some fungal and bacterial diseases, along with some pests, are airborne and so can blow into the garden.
- Plant waste that is destined for composting could be diseased and so the disease could spread through the composting process. This can include the contamination of soil from any leachate from the compost heap.
- Assisted spread — many pests and pathogens are spread by people on clothing or on tools or work boots.

In a recent survey, 40 per cent of the people walking around a public garden had phytophthora on their boots.

Positive interventions that can be included within Garden Health Plans could include:

- Informed plant selections.
- Good husbandry practices.
- Correct storage of growing media.
- Sterilisation of recirculating irrigation water.
- Pots and trays being sterilised between uses.
- Regular scouting.
- Development of a plant record system to record plant failures cross-referenced to planting sites and suppliers.
- Recording of plant passport information.
- Reviewing supplier biosecurity policies.
- Seeking advice when problems are identified.
- Practise integrated pest management.
- Train staff to be able to positively identify pests and diseases.
- Be able to differentiate pests from beneficial insects.
- Clean boots and shoes with water and then sterilise with Propellar or a similar product after visiting other gardens.

From a biosecurity perspective, boots worn in one garden should be scrubbed and sanitized before walking in a second garden, to prevent the spread of soil-borne pathogens.

- Clean tools between and during use, then sterilise with a product such as Propellar.
- Control vectors that spread viral diseases, such as aphids.
- Control secondary hosts for pests and diseases.
- Grow productive plants early, so they have cropped before pest numbers build up.
- Put up nesting boxes to increase the population of blue tits, which feed on plant pests.
- Practise good water hygiene by having clean gutters that feed clean water butts.
- Avoid problem plant species.
- Avoid impulse plant purchasing.
- Avoid procuring plants grown outside of the country.
- Grow plants with resistance to pests and diseases, for example, Sarpo potatoes are resistant to late blight.
- Check to ensure that all new plant material is healthy before bringing it into the garden.
- Anticipate the arrival of specific pests, such as gooseberry sawfly.
- Carry out operations at the right time, for example, pruning at the correct time of the year.

- Use barriers to keep pests off certain plants, for example, netting to protect fruit from birds or brassicas from cabbage white butterflies.

The Car Boot Threat

Xylella is a potential bacterial plant disease that has been identified in some EU countries. Plant health professionals have instigated a range of measures to reduce the risk of it being imported into the UK on plants for planting. *Xylella* is present in the sap of infected plant species; the bacterium can block the xylem, the water-conducting tissue in the plant, causing the appearance of wilting.

- In the USA without intervention, it is able to naturally spread 20km (12 miles) a year.
- 300 plant species can carry the disease, with six major taxa being classed as high risk.

- The method of control is to identify contaminated areas.
- To then eradicate all plant material that can carry *Xylella* within 100m of the outbreak, along with the control of vectors that can spread the infection.
- There will also be measures taken to reduce the risk of the *Xylella* spreading in a buffer zone, which could be up to 5km (3 miles). The UK Plant Health Portal (Defra) states that these measures would lead to environmental and social impacts. These would impact on both plant producers and those who manage gardens.
- Other regions outside the buffer zone are considered to be *Xylella*-free.

One of the key risks to the UK is plant material that has been imported for sale at car boot sales, especially olive trees, which have bypassed the plant health and phytosanitary protocols.

Old supermarket baskets can make effective barriers to prevent birds damaging young plants.

Rethinking is required. The cane can be replaced with a garden-grown support, the plastic pot with a terracotta one and the plastic netting either reused each year, or sustainable netting can be used.

The Emerging Importance of Biostimulants

Plant biostimulants contain either substances or microorganisms that benefit the plant. Biostimulants are often used to increase nutrient uptake, to increase tolerance to environmental stress or to improve/enhance plant quality.

Biostimulants can assist with nutrient uptake and assist with the use of those nutrients through the plant. Biostimulants include products such as seaweed extracts, which can improve abiotic stress tolerance and improve yield in productive growing.

The bark of willow trees is rich in salicylic acid. While we use refined forms of this active ingredient in aspirin, Cambridge University Botanic Garden suggests that salicylic acid has many functions within plants: it protects against infection through a range of antifungal and antibacterial qualities; it also has allelopathic effects, preventing the growth of some plant species close by; it is also used within plants to regulate flowering.

Willow bark also has high concentrations of hormones that promote adventitious root formation. Some plant propagators use willow water as a natural replacement for rooting powders.

Garlic is often used as a biostimulant, with the results of trials showing improved plant height, increased number of leaves and greater dry weight. Other studies have shown enhanced chlorophyll production and an increase in sugars in the plant sap. Garlic extracts have also been shown to mitigate stress. For example, Solufeed's Turf Energizer is garlic based, and is claimed to stimulate growth, vigour and tillering (production of low-growing side-shoots in grass), along with assisting in nutrient uptake.

It is important to establish and apply the plant procurement protocols, outlined in Chapter 4, to reduce the risk of introducing *Xylella* and other pathogens to the UK, and to planting sites:

- Always buy from established reputable businesses.
- Always ask for their biosecurity policy.
- Always ask for a plant passport number.
- Choose locally grown plants that are not imported from outside of the UK.

Creating Garden Health Plans

Garden Health Plans take into account every impact on plant health and consider how these impacts can integrate to cause more serious plant health threats. The first stage in creating a Garden Health Plan is to divide the garden up into zones that can be considered as one. Productive areas will have differing plant health risks to grassed areas or woodland gardens. The abiotic and biotic plant health risks can then be considered, with the staged intervention principles of IPM being considered.

The table below is an example that can be used to develop a working Garden Health Plan.

Garden Health Plans can also be developed as management documents, for example, with the inclusion of IPM stages.

Developing a Garden Health Plan

Garden Health Plan for:			
Introductory notes:			
Important information:			
Negative factors that impact on plant health (abiotic/biotic)	Ranked interventions		Reflection/review

Example extract from a Garden Health Plan

Garden Health Plan for:	Rose garden	
Introductory notes:	Carry out weekly inspections of roses in season, and monthly inspection of roses out of the growing season. List key areas of concern, there has been previous incidence of wind rock and blackspot. Year 1, record thresholds (identified as the point at which pest and disease damage deters from the aesthetic value of the area).	
Important information:	Rose cultivars are unknown, as they were planted unlabelled when the property was purchased.	
Negative factors that impact on plant health (abiotic/biotic)	Ranked interventions	Reflection/review
Blackspot	September–November, look for fallen leaves, collect and burn. November–December, apply a layer of organic mulch 70mm deep, pulled away from the stem of the rose to seal in any blackspot in the soil and prevent rain splash introducing the disease to young leaves in the spring. March, prune out all affected wood, and remove fallen leaves. Ensure good weed control, to ensure effective air movement through the plant. Leaves most susceptible when young. Disease requires water to grow and enter leaves, so avoid any irrigation over the leaves/irrigate early morning to allow leaves to dry before nightfall. Prune back overhanging shrub/tree branches to prevent drip on to leaves and allow more sun in to dry the leaves quickly after rain. Apply a blend of specialist rose mycorrhizal fungi, to aid with nutrient uptake. Trial with a chemical control of rose sulphur sprayed on new growth as directed to protect against spores of the disease. (Research if this could impact on mycorrhiza.)	Develop skills to positively identify blackspot on the stems of roses. Do not want to go down chemical control route (fungicide) as I want to establish mycorrhizal relationships in the soil. Would like to replace old roses with new cultivars that are resistant to blackspot, however rose replant disease would mean moving the rose garden to a new location. As the mitigations shown were not totally effective last year, I am adding sulphur to the mix this year as a trial. Have improved airflow to the plant, and more thorough pruning. Have read that Polenta, (cornmeal) scattered around roses and worked into the top 25mm of the soil can promote Trichoderma, a beneficial fungus, which offers protection against blackspot. Will try this on 50 per cent of my plants next year as a trial. If blackspot continues to be an issue, perhaps consider removing the rose garden, as it also requires irrigation. Are these the right plants for the site?
Leafcutter bees	No action required as the bees are also beneficial and important from a biodiversity context.	Positive identification. Applying the retrain my eyes approach, and learn to love the holes as signs that the garden is home to leafcutter bees and benefitting biodiversity.
Large rose sawfly	Scout. The damage is not life-threatening to the rose, and the larvae are food for wild birds and other predators. Scouting can reveal eggs laid in linear scars; it is possible to kill these by dragging a nail down the scar. Can pick off the larvae, if there appears to be a lot of damage. If damage is mild, then leave. Alternative is to use a spray of water to wash the larvae off the rose.	Positive identification. Small infestations have been on one of two branches, which were pruned off. This has worked for the last two seasons. The water spray was effective last year at washing larvae off the rose.

Wind rock	November — prune the shrub roses by 30 per cent to reduce height and so reduce wind rock over the winter. Check weekly and after high winds to ensure that further pruning is not required.	Roses in exposed location have rocked in the winter. One rose died after water froze in the hole, crushing the stem of the rose.
Aphids	Scout. When aphid numbers start to build up, rinse off with a directed jet of water. Underplant the rose with garlic, evidence suggests that the garlic will protect the rose from aphids.	Positive identification. Tolerating some aphids on the roses has not reduced flowering. On weekly inspection if the numbers are rising, then a spray of water washes the stem clean. It is hard to establish the effectiveness of the garlic but will continue to use this as a space to grow garlic.
Weed control	No action required, this problem was resolved by mulching deeply and avoiding soil cultivation.	Weeds were tolerated under the roses to 200mm in height, when they start to grow taller, they are possibly reducing airflow and so can exacerbate black spot. The use of mulch topped-up annually, has eliminated weed growth.

A Garden Health Plan with the inclusion of IPM stages

Garden Health Plan for:									
Introductory notes:									
Important information:									
Negative factors that impact on plant health (abiotic/biotic)	Ranked interventions	IPM stages							Reflection/review
		1	2	3	4	5	6	7	

Final Reflections

- Why is action required?
- When is the best time to carry out control?
- Will the control have wider impacts on biodiversity?
- Can I identify the pathway for introduction?
- Could I have managed the process better?
- Have I kept all documentation, i.e. plant passports?

CHAPTER 6

SUSTAINABLE LAWN MANAGEMENT

Study nature, love nature, stay close to nature. It will never fail you.

Frank Lloyd Wright

Francis Bacon stated, 'nothing is more pleasant to the eye than green grass kept finely shorn'. There is an undoubted truth in this statement, as lawns have become a popular part of almost every garden. Lawn care, or turf management, is a specialist area of horticulture, which often involves considerable inputs of fertilizer, herbicide and maintenance with equipment that is powered with fossil fuel. These practices are problematic from a sustainability perspective. There are emerging models that suggest that lawns can be managed to reflect sustainable principles.

Lawns offer a number of ecosystem services:

- Functional
    - Lawns can reduce ambient temperatures.
    - Lawns filter and remove particulate matter for air and water.
    - Lawns offer a relatively low-cost surface.
    - Lawns are more ecologically appropriate than gravel, paving or concrete.
    - Lawns offer carbon sequestration.

The lawns at Levens Hall, in Cumbria, leading the eye through the garden and providing a foil to the plantings.

- Aesthetic
  - Lawns make excellent foils for plantings.
  - Lawns are a restful colour and pleasing to the eye.
- Recreational
  - Lawns make excellent play areas for children.
  - Turfgrass makes unrivalled sporting surfaces.
- Social
  - Lawns reduce noise pollution in urban areas.
  - Lawns bring people together to play games and picnic.
- Economic
  - The lawn and turfcare industry provides permanent secure employment for a considerable number of people.
- Well-being
  - The green colour of lawns is restful and restorative to the eye.
  - Playing informal lawn games and sports helps meet exercise and movement goals.

These benefits of lawns and turfgrass surfaces are balanced by the negative impacts of lawncare:

- Mowing with petrol-powered equipment.
- Creation of noise pollution.
- Use of fertilizers.
- Use of herbicides.
- Use of water to irrigate.

Sustainable lawn management is a process that enhances the range of ecosystem services that lawns and grassed areas offer, while reducing the negative aspects, to create net-positive garden spaces.

Despite all the work involved in maintaining them, lawns are still one of the most popular of garden features.

Mowing

Mowing using a petrol lawnmower has been shown to be one of the most environmentally damaging aspects of garden maintenance; with some reports suggesting that mowing a lawn for one hour with a petrol mower produces similar emissions to driving 148km (93 miles). There are also reports of lawnmowers, in good running order, being taken to MOT test stations to monitor their emissions; these were so high that they could not be determined. Mowing lawns with petrol-based equipment is problematic from a health and safety perspective, as the emissions pose a risk to the operator. Part of the development of risk assessments is to favour the safest method of working to eliminate risk. It can, therefore, be argued that electrical equipment should be favoured in the mitigation of risk. If this is not practicable, then from health and safety and sustainability perspectives, the most basic mitigations would be to ensure equipment is maintained to manufacturer recommendations. Other mitigations can include considering alternative and less polluting fuels. The current move in the UK to E10 petrol is causing many issues as the fuel is hydroscopic. The key impact is on the starting of equipment when the fuel has been stored in a vented container or fuel tank for a few weeks. One alternative that is used by a growing number of professional horticulturists is to change to alkylate petrol fuel. As well as coming premixed (which helps to increase engine life and reduce breakdown) these fuels are not hydroscopic and do not 'go off'. Aspen, one of the alkylate fuel brands, identifies health benefits linked to these fuels being free of benzene and olefins, which are both carcinogenic.

However, fuels such as Aspen, while being less damaging to the environment, are far from sustainable. Alkylate petrols are produced from excess gasses produced in the distillation of crude oil and so, while they are the cleanest and least polluting fuel available, they still emit carbon in considerable quantities. In most cases the fuel is supplied in 5ltr plastic containers, which add to the environmental footprint.

From a sustainability perspective, and social, economic and environmental considerations, there can be no doubt that there is no place for tools that are powered by hydrocarbon fuels in sustainable garden management. It is important, when considering the replacement of hydrocarbon-powered tools, to consider the full lifetime environmental impact of

It has been estimated that one hour of mowing produces the equivalent emissions to driving 157km (98 miles) in a small car.

replacement equipment to include manufacture, operation, servicing and end of life disposal.

Generally, human-powered machines are the least damaging of all to the environment. Modern human-powered lawnmowers, while they may not be appropriate for large lawns in public parks and gardens, are a viable alternative for smaller to medium-sized gardens. The design of these pieces of equipment has been considerably improved in recent years. If used correctly, the input of user energy is not significantly more than is used in the operation of a self-propelled petrol lawnmower.

Corded electrical equipment offers sustainability advantages over battery-powered as this eliminates the sourcing of materials for batteries, the emissions from battery manufacture and the potential issues with regard to recycling considerations at end of life. The environmental credentials of corded equipment are increased when powered by electricity produced on-site from solar panels or supplied from renewable sources, such as green tariffs.

Battery-powered equipment, especially when one buys into a battery ecosystem, is the next logical option; it is not as sustainable as corded, but it is considerably more sustainable than equipment powered by hydrocarbon fuels. Buying into a battery ecosystem allows a small number of batteries to be used to power several units. Lithium-ion batteries have facilitated the development of a new generation of electrical power tools, which offer the same or increased levels of power to petrol. Tree surgeons are adopting top handle lithium-ion battery chainsaws, and there are now a wide range of pedestrian and ride-on battery lawn-mowers available for both amateur and professional use. Fast-charge battery technology has made these options even more attractive. The ideal scenario is for one battery to be recharging, while the other is discharging.

Advantages of Electrically Powered Mowers

Research carried out in the USA has identified the key advantages of electrically powered mowers over petrol ones as follows:

- Electric mowers emit 3,300 times less hydrocarbons.
- Electric mowers emit 5,000 times less CO_2.
- Electric mowers emit 80 per cent less NO_2.

Nutrition

Having considered mowing equipment, the focus can now move to the next most damaging aspect of turf care. In Chapter 4, the concept of fertilizers negatively impacting on the soil ecosystem was introduced. There are a number of different approaches being devised to replace the use of traditional fertilizers in sustainable lawn management. Peter Korn, the Swedish plantsman and designer, advocates throwing weeds removed from borders on to the lawn, and then running a mulching mower over the surface of the grass. This is an interesting concept. Mulching mowers cut the arisings (grass clippings) from mowing into small particles, which are forced down into the grass. This practice was at one time considered to encourage the growth of thatch; however, current thinking does not support this theory. It can be argued that returning arisings from mowing to the soil creates a circular economy. Plant nutrients taken up by roots and so lost from the soil, are lost from the leaves in the mowing process. These are returned during mowing, thus eliminating the need for feeding, the mulched weeds adding to the nutrient status of the lawn. Other horti-culturists are advocating the development of biostimulants to reduce stress in lawns and to increase their resilience to lawn diseases. These products often contain garlic and selenium. Selenium is an essential element and so is arguably a fertilizer. However, low rates of application of selenium have been shown to have a positive effect on the appearance and the health of grass. The selenium antagonises the grass, which responds to this antagonism by producing a slightly thicker cuticle layer, which makes the grass appear to have sheen. The thicker cuticle also offers the grass protection from fungal spores.

Weed Control

Weed control within sustainable lawn management is a complex area. The term weed itself is problematic as it suggests a plant that is out of place, and this may not always be the case. Thinking of lawn weeds as spontaneous plants that reduce the negative impacts of lawns, which are monocultures of one plant spe-cies, may offer a different perspective. The benefits of a diverse lawn area can be considerable. A deciding factor with regard to maintenance is likely to be the purpose of the grassed area. It would be entirely appropriate for a putting green to be kept weed-free;

however, it may be more appropriate for a utility lawn to be more biodiverse. This concept allows the setting of action thresholds, which were introduced in Chapter 5.

There is little doubt that the most effective method of weed control is the length and frequency of cut. To that end, robotic lawnmowers, which benefit from lithium-ion batteries, can be programmed to cut the grass daily. This practice removes top growth from any non-grass species, exhausting the roots, which will lead to the death of most broad-leaved lawn weeds. Some of the spreading weeds, such as *Ranunculus repens* (creeping buttercup), *Lotus coniculatus* (bird's foot trefoil) or *Prunella vulgaris* (selfheal) are more problematic to control, as they are low growing and often escape the blades of the lawnmower. These can still be controlled in a sustainable way. Lawn rakes can be used to lift the weeds prior to mowing. This simple technique is surprisingly effective, as is the ancient technique of cutting a hashtag-shaped pattern in the turf affected by the weed and then raking, thus reducing the size of the weed to the part of the hashtag where the weed roots. Other control measures include the gradual digging out of perennial weeds such as *Rumex obtusifolius* (broad-leaved dock) or *Taraxacum officianale* (dandelion). Gardeners who are used to using spot treatments of herbicide from a trigger pack, can replace the herbicide with a flask of boiling water or one of the new acetic acid herbicides that are coming on to the market for a less damaging chemical-based control option.

A matter of perspective. Beautiful wildflowers – or problem weeds. It's all down to the lens we use to view our garden.

Irrigation

Water is far from being a renewable resource. A changing climate with prolonged periods of drought will result in increasingly tight restrictions on water usage. It is also significant that the time that water is required in horticulture, is when it is in shortest supply. The irrigation of lawns has no place in a sustainable garden. The effects of drought on a lawn can be limited by raising the height of cut; this practice can result in deeper root formation. These larger, deeper roots are better able to extract water from the soil profile. It is also worth noting that grass is a theatrical plant. It responds to drought conditions by spectacularly turning yellow. Only in extreme conditions does this threaten to kill the grass; most lawns return to green shortly after rainfall. Indeed, this process of yellowing is a natural survival strategy that early grass species developed to survive dry summers.

Those working in public gardens often irrigate early in the morning in drought conditions as their visitors enjoy the spectacle of verdant green lawns. More sustainable practices, such as eliminating irrigation, may require interpretation to explain why the lawn is looking yellow.

An interpretation board could explain the impacts of watering lawns.

Messaging such as this is important in allowing visitors to understand why maintenance practices have changed. It also allows visitors to understand and engage in your sustainability journey.

Reduced Inputs

One of the most significant ways of reducing the carbon footprint and boosting the biodiversity impact of a grassed area is to reduce the cutting regime. We normally cut grass to 30—35mm (1½in) with the golden rule being to remove no more that 10mm (½in) of growth (30 per cent) at any one time. This length of sward is ideal as it allows the lawn to have sufficient area of leaf to ensure effective photosynthesis, which produces the carbohydrates necessary for growth, a good level of tillering (where side shoots come out of the grass plant, so producing a mat of growth) and a good level of weed control.

Reducing the area of lawn cut is one way to reduce inputs, especially if the lawnmower is petrol-powered. This can be achieved by widening flower beds (allowing more extensive layered planting within the garden, which provides ecosystem services) or by reducing maintenance to simply cutting paths through the lawn and mowing an edge strip on a weekly basis. Other areas of grass can be mown on a fortnightly or even monthly basis. Reducing the cutting of the lawn by 50 per cent will reduce the carbon footprint of mowing by 50 per cent.

Did you know, applying 25mm of irrigation water to one hectare of lawn, uses up a staggering 296 cubic metres of water?

That is enough water to fill 296 000 litre bottles!

Last year the water we used to irrigate this lawn would fill a total of 1 420 000 litre bottles of water!

We consider this to be unstainable.

We are therefore allowing our lawns to naturally adapt to the drought by turning yellow and sleeping through summer.

They will green up almost immediately when it rains.

An example interpretation board.

Repairing/Establishing a New Lawn

While it is tempting to repair areas of damaged lawn, or to establish new lawns with turf, this is less sustainable than seed. The cultivation of turf requires inputs of land, irrigation, mowing and, finally, lifting. The fields of establishing turf offer a limited range of ecosystem services. The transport of turf is also energy intensive. Having identified these limitations, turf can still be considered to be a very useful product in a wide range of horticultural situations. From a sustainability perspective, seed should be our first choice when repairing and establishing lawn areas.

Pests and Pathogens

Grassed areas can experience the occurrence of lawn pests and diseases. The key to managing and controlling these is to consider them as important parts of a Garden Health Plan, where all the contributory factors to their establishment are considered, with remedial actions following the eight steps of Integrated Pest Management.

It is worth noting that the reduced fertilizer inputs and applications of biostimulants should reduce the incidence of some diseases of lawn turf, while there are effective nematode controls (biological control) of some lawn pests. These biological controls are often impacted by soils containing pesticide residues; however, this is not the case within sustainable gardens, allowing these organisms to give more effective control.

Rethinking Our Grassed Areas

There has never been a better time to fundamentally rethink the purposes our lawns are designed to fulfil and to consider how they can be developed to offer the wide range of ecosystem services, while also playing a significant part in the restoration of biodiversity. Statistics released by Plantlife, a UK charity, show just how significant our lawns can be for wildflowers, pollinators and invertebrates.

- The average UK garden is 196m^2.
- In an average garden, 50 per cent or 98m^2 of its entire area is lawn.

- We have lost 97 per cent of all species-rich grassland in the last ninety years.
- The total area of species-rich grassland lost in the UK is 1.5 times the size of Wales.

In December 2021, Natural History Museum data indicated the UK as being one of the world's most nature-depleted countries, with only 53 per cent of its biodiversity left. This is well below the global average of 75 per cent.

Sustainable lawn management is designed to meet the needs of all users, including pollinators, invertebrates and people. The key changes in management practices do not require the digging out of lawns. It just requires the adoption of more informed management regimes. Sustainable lawn management reduces carbon and water footprints. It boosts biodiversity.

Through their citizen science project 'every flower counts', Plantlife have been able to establish a considerable amount of data to suggest best practice with regard to how we could change our lawn-management strategies to enhance biodiversity, reduce our carbon footprint and even sequester carbon.

Plantlife's data indicate that, while the majority of lawns in the UK support one to five honeybees per square metre, some were able to support closer to twenty or even twenty-five honeybees per square metre. If we are to use our garden to benefit biodiversity, it is worth considering the characteristics of gardens that have the highest score. These gardens included significant areas of grass that were cut monthly. The mowing removes the competition from surrounding grass, allowing air and light to get to wildflowers that may otherwise be shaded out. The flowers growing in these monthly mown areas had high nectar outputs. The nectar output can be measured in micrograms of nectar produced each day. The research found *Bellis perennis* (daisies) offer pollinators around 3,000µg of nectar a day, while *Taraxacum officinale* (dandelions) offer over 7,000µg with *Trifolium repens* (white clover) coming in with an impressive 135,000µg. Another critical factor was allowing some areas of grass to continue to grow unmown, with just one single cut taking place in late summer after flowering had finished. These areas had fewer wildflowers but offered a habitat to a wider range of invertebrates.

The sustainable gardener could apply these principles to produce an attractive area of lawn, enriched

Trifolium repens (white clover), *Crisium palustre* (marsh thistle) and *Erica carnea/Calluna vulgaris* (heather) together contribute almost 50 per cent to the national nectar provision.

with wildflowers selected for the timing and the volume of their nectar supply. This lawn could be mown monthly, with wildflowers quickly re-blooming after cutting. Mowing less frequently leads to a decline in these species, as the grass shades out the sunlight. However, other species such as knapweed and red clover tend to establish in this longer grass.

The optimum lawn would, therefore, be one where approximately 50 per cent of the area is mown on a monthly, rather than weekly basis. Areas of long grass can then be framed by these mown paths and play areas, thus making the longer grass look intentional and allowing it to become a feature of the garden.

Our eyes need to be retrained when viewing our lawns. On a personal note, I have spent many a year battling with bird's foot trefoil in my lawn. It has managed to survive every strategy to bring about its demise.

However, when rethinking the concept of what a lawn could be, research was undertaken. Bird's foot trefoil is an important source of nectar and is a food source for approximately 140 species. One can change perspective and apply a lens of sustainability, viewing what was an infuriating weed as a pantry supporting the food needs of a wide biodiverse group of animals that call your garden home.

Perennial Meadows

The logical next step for our grassed areas is to allow them to become species-rich perennial meadows. There is an important distinction to be made here between a perennial meadow and an annual one. Annual meadows, which can be inspired by cornfields, require reseeding every year. Many of the seed

The Yorkshire Arboretum reduced mowings to create pathways for visitors to access their collection of trees. Wildflowers, including orchids, just appeared in the unmown grass, which is controlled with yellow rattle.

Rhinanthus minor (yellow rattle) – Nature's lawnmower.

growth of grasses. This gives wildflowers an advantage. It is an annual plant that is best sown from fresh seed in the late autumn, as it requires chilling to enable germination in the spring. The young plants extend their roots into the soil and into the roots of other neighbouring plants where they extract water and nutrients. The impact of this process, according to Plantlife, is a reduction of 60 per cent in the growth of grasses, hence the name 'meadow maker' or 'nature's lawnmower'. Yellow rattle is an annual plant but sets seed easily to allow it to survive year to year. It can be problematic to establish. This is often the result of old seed being sold. It is worth asking those who have it established if you can collect some hay in early autumn, drying the hay and then shaking the seeds out over the grassed area to be sown a few weeks later. Yellow rattle is also available as a plug plant.

This concept of borrowing plants to establish a meadow is often used, with hay cut from one meadow being transported to where a new meadow is to be established. The hay is spread to allow the seeds to fall and can then be removed. This simple low-cost method of creating new perennial meadows is established with minimum input and intervention.

Six golden rules when establishing a perennial wildflower meadow:

1. Test your soil to see if it is acidic or alkaline, and then choose an appropriate plant species to suit the site.
2. Sow the meadow with fresh, local provenance seed, to ensure that the plants are best suited for the local climate.
3. An alternative to sowing wildflower seeds is to purchase plug plants, which can be planted within the meadow, and often establish better than seed.
4. Minimal intervention is the key; perennial wildflower meadows, once established, require no pesticides, no herbicides and no fertilizers.
5. Cut the meadow once in late summer/early autumn. An Austrian scythe is often the preferred tool for this. Leave the cut grass for a few days to allow seeds to fall and then take away for composting or other uses.
6. Take part in Plantlife's 'every flower counts' as a way of recording the species that are growing well and for calculating your own personal nectar score (PNS).

catalogues tempting us with wildflower mixes contain annual plants such as *Centaurea cyanus* (cornflower) or *Daucus carota* (wild carrot); these mixes can look spectacular and provide a wide range of ecosystem services but the major limitation is the requirement for annual seeding.

Perennial meadows are a complex matrix of lawn grasses left to grow or can include more appropriate species such as *Cynosurus cristatus* (crested dog's tail) and the sweet vanilla-tasting *Anthoxanthum odoratum* (sweet vernal grass), both of which are food plants of many butterfly caterpillars, including the skipper family. Another great grass to plant within a perennial meadow is *Holcus lanatus* (Yorkshire fog), which is much loved by rabbits, has lovely purple flower heads and is a food plant of several butterflies, including the skippers.

Introducing Nature's Lawnmower

The enemy of many wildflowers is a rich soil, which encourages the growth of grass species, which then shade out and smother wildflowers. *Rhinanthus minor* (yellow rattle) is partially parasitic and so stunts the

Perfect Plants for an Annually Cut Perennial Meadow

Anthyllis vulneraria (Kidney Vetch)

Anthyllis vulneraria. CAROLINE JACKSON

Origin: UK.
Description: Small, yellow flowers, sitting on fluffy cushions.
Height: Grows to 30cm (12in).
Flowering season: Flowers throughout the summer months, June to September.
Ecosystem services: It is the only food source for the caterpillars of the small blue butterfly.

Leucanthemum vulgare (Oxeye Daisy)

Origin: Europe, Central Asia.
Description: The flowers look similar to daisies but are up to 60mm (2½in) in diameter.

Leucanthemum vulgare.

Height: 0.5–1.5m (1¼–5ft).
Flowering season: Flowers May to September.
Ecosystem services: Wide range of pollinators supported, including butterflies, bees and hoverflies.

Plantago lanceolata (Ribwort Plantain)

Plantago lanceolata.

Origin: Native to Europe.
Description: The flowers are black/brown with cream/yellow anthers.
Height: 0.5m (1¼ft).
Flowering season: April to October.
Ecosystem services: Flowers provide nectar to pollinating insects; the seed heads provide food for goldfinches over winter.

Trifolium pratense (Red Clover)

Trifolium pratense.

Origin: Native to Europe.
Description: The flowers are pink to red in colour. Has a strong taproot and is resistant to drought. Often used in agriculture, as it has root nodules that convert nitrogen from the air into nitrates that crops can use.
Height: 0.5m (1¼ft).
Flowering season: Flowers from late spring into early autumn.
Ecosystem services: Flowers offer high levels of nectar and support a wide range of species. It is also a food plant for certain species of caterpillar.

Lotus corniculatus (Bird's Foot Trefoil)

Lotus corniculatus.

Origin: Native to Europe.
Description: Member of the pea family, low growing, small, yellow, pea-like flowers with deeper orange veins.
Height: 35cm (13½in).

Flowering season: Flowers from May to September.
Ecosystem services: A food source for over 140 species. Important food plant of caterpillars of common blue, silver-studded blue and wood white (unusual species of butterfly regarded as priority species under the UK Post 2010 Biodiversity Framework).

Vicia cracca (Tufted Vetch)

Vicia cracca.

Origin: Native to Europe.
Description: Lilac-coloured flowers, leaves have tendrils to support the plant and allow it to climb up grass.
Height: 30cm (11½in).
Flowering season: Summer.
Ecosystem services: Food plant for beetles, weevils, caterpillars and pollinators.

Taraxacum officinale (Dandelion)

Taraxacum officinale.

Origin: Persia.
Description: The yellow flowers, once thought of as lawn weeds, are now a sign of a sustainable lawn that is doing good.
Height: 35cm (13½in).
Flowering season: Spring into summer.
Ecosystem services: Very important early food plant for butterflies, bumblebees, day-flying moths, hover-flies and solitary bees amongst many others.

Viola odorata (Wood Violet)

Viola odorata.

Origin: Europe and Asia.
Description: Violet-blue flowers, with five oval petals. Suitable for shady edges of meadows.
Height: 6cm (2¼in).
Flowering season: April.
Ecosystem services: Food source for butterflies in woodland hedgerow habitats.

Cruciata laevipes (Crosswort)

Cruciata laevipes.

Origin: UK.
Description: Frothy small green/yellow flowers that start compact and space out as the plant grows taller during the year.
Height: 0.50m (1¼ft).
Flowering season: June to September.
Ecosystem services: The flowers are a source of pollen and nectar for numerous species.

Cardamine pratensis (Cuckoo Flower/Milkmaids)

Cardamine pratensis.

Origin: Europe, Western Asia.
Description: Pale-pink flowers on slender stalks.
Height: 0.50m (1¼ft).
Flowering season: April to June.
Ecosystem services: Food plant to orange tip butterflies.
Flowers pollinated by bees, moths and butterflies.

CHAPTER 7

PRINCIPLES OF PRUNING

Less is more.

Ludwig Mies Van Der Rohe

The lens of sustainability prompts a change of perspective and provides the opportunity to be sustainable in every gardening task. To that end, when the sustainable gardener is pruning, they are not just considering the basic principles — the 4 Ds of pruning:

- Remove all **dead** wood to promote plant health.
- Remove all **diseased** wood to promote plant health.
- Remove all **damaged** wood to promote plant health.
- Remove all **duplicated** wood to improve form.

They are also applying the three pillars of sustainability to the pruning process: social, economic and environmental.

Putting Sustainability First When Buying Garden Tools

One of the first areas to consider is the sustainability of the tools that we are using. This includes considering the following criteria:

- While plastic components in tools are not, by definition, single-use plastics, it is more sustainable to choose tools that use minimal plastic. Garden tools that are made of wood and forged from metal tend to have a greater longevity than those made with plastic components.
- Choose tools with carbon steel blades that can be sharpened.
- Choose the highest quality of tool that your budget allows.
- If the budget is restricted, then consider second-hand tools. Those from the 1920s–50s are often exceptionally well made and have a wonderful patina of age.
- Very high-quality tools with replaceable parts could be a much more sustainable option.
- Research the brand: does the brand have a sustainability policy?
- Does the brand provide evidence that it treats its people well and pays them fairly?

Rethinking Pruning

Applying sustainable thinking to horticultural operations involves developing a deeper understanding of the process. It involves considering a number of

All products we purchase involve five main life-cycle stages: material extraction, manufacturing, packaging and transportation, use and end of life.

sometimes conflicting factors. How does the pruning process of the climber impact on plant health, on flower production and on the wider range of ecosystem services provided? New approaches to pruning should consider this wider range of factors, with techniques developed to suit site conditions and the individual plants under cultivation. Instead of applying a strict principle, 'prune, by one-third in November, and then reduce the growth to half the original height in March', the sustainable gardener takes a more relaxed, or nuanced, approach. Is the plant still in active growth in November? (It is worth noting that much of the published information on pruning is based on weather patterns and temperatures from the 1970s and 1990s. A fast-changing climate requires a rethinking of the timing of many maintenance operations.) Is it appropriate to leave some growth and dead flower heads to overwinter, as these provide overwintering sites for invertebrates? Pruning practice is the result of

Case Study: Secateurs

Many professional horticulturists use secateurs, but which of the leading manufacturers offer a sustainable choice?

A search of a number of websites of leading tool companies has been carried out. Many companies had little information with regard to sustainability. One company, Felco, used their website to explain their commitment to sustainability with the following information:

- Secateurs and pruning shears are made of 50 per cent recycled aluminium.
- All parts are replaceable and so the tool can, theoretically, last forever.
- There are performance indicators that measure and compare the water and electricity consumed in making each tool. The carbon footprint of each tool is measured. These figures are reviewed annually to inform the improvement, design and investment processes.
- All electricity used is from renewable sources, some is generated on-site using solar panels on the factory roof. It takes 1.71Kw/h of electricity to make one pair of pruning shears.

- Waste heat is recovered from equipment and water is reused.
- Phthalates (toxic chemicals used to soften PVC) have been eliminated from the manufacture of tools.
- Employees are given financial incentives to move to the village where the factory is located to reduce the environmental impacts of commuting — 27 per cent of employees now live in the village where the factory is located.
- Felco support environmental projects and have beehives producing their own honey on the factory roof.

Other horticultural tool suppliers are moving to become carbon neutral.

All Sneeboer horticultural tools are energy neutral, with the 96,000Kw of energy used being generated by solar panels on the roof of the factory.

Information with a similar level of detail could not be accessed at the time of the search from other manufacturers' websites. Contacting preferred tool suppliers and asking how their processes compare highlights the issue of sustainability and can result in information being shared and practices improved.

factual information relating to whether the plant flowers on this year's wood or old wood. The health status of the plant, the way the plant has responded to previous pruning and the impact of pruning on biodiversity, are also worthy of consideration. Pruning decisions are based on weaving many strands of thinking together to gently guide and steer the whole garden in the right direction.

Rethinking process involves a re-evaluation of the 4 Ds introduced at the start of this chapter to ascertain if these are still applicable as absolute rules within a sustainable garden.

Remove All Dead Wood to Promote Plant Health

While, from a plant health perspective, it is better to remove all dead wood, dead wood can also perform a number of important functions within gardens. The dead wood may be host to species of lichen, moss or fungi. Beetle larvae live within dead wood. Dead wood can also be an important habitat for wild birds, with woodpeckers and willow tits needing dead wood for both feeding and nesting.

Carefully considered judgement-calls are required. Shall this dead wood be left on this tree? Decisions should be made with reference to the wider Garden Health Plan. As part of this plan, scouting and monitoring are required, which can result in annual (or more frequent) inspection of the dead wood being carried out to ensure that it is posing a minimal health risk to

surrounding plants. It is also important to ascertain that it poses no health and safety risk to people. It may be that professional advice should be sought from an arborist to help inform health and safety decisions. Ascertaining the cause of dieback should be part of the investigation carried out when developing the Garden Health Plan.

An unmanaged, natural woodland can be made up of 25 per cent dead wood.

Remove All Diseased Wood to Promote Plant Health

The decisions regarding diseased growth should be informed by the holistic approach to garden health that has been researched and identified in the Garden Health Plan. It is important to understand the disease, the seasons when infection can occur, and the speed and severity of attack. This allows for a nuanced, risk-based approach to managing health during pruning. Some diseases, such as canker on apple trees, which is caused by the fungus *Neonectria ditissima,* spreads by producing two types of spore. Water-dispersed spores tend to be produced over the summer, allowing the canker to creep and spread to neighbouring branches on the same tree. This also means that if pruning is carried out while these spores are being carried in water on the surface of the bark, there is a high risk of infecting new pruning cuts, on this or neighbouring trees. Sterilising tools regularly and between trees is recommended. If the canker is being left for

Dead wood is often left, either on trees or as standing dead wood, to provide ecosystem services. If the tree is large, an arborist should be consulted to ensure the dead wood poses no risk.

observation to map its damage, perhaps because it is on a main branch or the trunk of the tree and removal may kill or adversely impact on the tree, then it is important to ensure that there are no lesions or pruning cuts immediately below the canker, which could allow further opportunities for infection. A second type of spore is released in the winter or the spring. These spores travel in the wind, with neighbouring apple trees most at risk. Pruning decisions should take into account a range of factors, for example, whether neighbouring trees are resistant or susceptible to apple canker, their distance from the infected plant, the prevailing wind direction and whether there are susceptible apples in neighbouring gardens. Growth that is pruned out may be infectious and should not be composted within the garden. It should be bagged to prevent spore release and transported to an off-site composting facility. These composting facilities utilise hot heaps that reach peak temperatures that will kill spores, ensuring that the resulting compost will not pose a plant health risk.

Other fungal diseases that can appear on dead or dying branches do not pose as severe a risk to plant health and can become part of the ecology of the garden. *Auricularia auricula-judae* (jelly ear) is a charming fungus, often found on *Sambucus nigra* (elderberry). This edible fungus is itself a food source for wildlife. (Note: while it is regarded as edible and is described as like eating a rubber with bones in it, no fungus should be eaten or tasted unless there is a 100 per cent accurate identification by an expert.)

Remove All Damaged Wood to Promote Plant Health

Generally, the removal of damaged wood is considered as part of a Garden Health Plan. Damaged wood, as well as being unsightly, can provide entry points for fungal and bacterial infections. It should be noted, however, that trees and woody plants have effective mechanisms to protect them from infections and so it is not always necessary, or appropriate, to remove damaged wood in every circumstance. While it may be appropriate to remove a branch that always gets hit by a passing vehicle, there are other situations in which the removal of the branch or damaged wood might impact on animal habitat, for example reducing the nesting or roosting potential of a site. In such cases,

Auricularia auricula-judae or jelly ear.

carefully considered judgements need to be made. The decisions taken are then documented in the Garden Health Plan, to allow careful review over time to inform future pruning decisions.

Top Tip

It should be added that while keeping records may seem impractical, they do offer a valuable insight to the speed and severity of plant diseases. With the advent of smartphones, the documentation can be images captured on the phone and imported into the Garden Health Plan, to allow a visual assessment of how the damage looked the previous year. The keeping of records allows a more nuanced approach to plant health management than the application of strict rules that may not apply in every instance. For example, the plant health risk for fungal disease is greater in the damper, western areas of the UK, than the drier, eastern areas, as leaves in the wet have a film of moisture on them for longer periods.

Remove All Duplicated Wood to Improve Form

This fourth 'D' involves the potential removal of branches to improve the aesthetic of a tree or shrub. The removal of this otherwise healthy wood may be appropriate for the early formative pruning of a specimen tree, or for fruit trees. However, removing duplicating branches from bushes or trees in other settings, such as in woodland gardens, may not be necessary, unless the Garden Health Plan has, for example, identified this species as being susceptible to fungal disease and instructs thinning of canopies to allow for increased air movement to evaporate the film of water on the leaf, and so reduce the risk of fungal infection. The management of this risk should be considered holistically, as the removal of the branch will reduce the photosynthetic area, which impacts on growth. Other wider considerations, for example the impact of removing leaves from an important host plant to caterpillars, have wider impacts on the ecology and biodiversity of the area.

The Rule Is, There Are No Rules

It should be stressed that as rules are being re-evaluated and considered from a wider perspective, there are fewer absolutes. Instead, there are tentative decisions, which require close observation and recording to inform future actions.

Climate change, the results of citizen science projects and horticultural research, inform best practice. Older gardening books offer historical insights, but do not reflect current thinking.

Planned Interventions

It is important to have a clear plan and purpose in mind prior to pruning.

Is the aim:

- Formative pruning?
- To remove disease?
- To remove the previous year's unwanted growth?
- To increase airflow?
- To contain the plant?
- To encourage flowering?
- To create habitat?

Timing Pruning Interventions

The timing of pruning can have a significant impact on biodiversity. Pruning back herbaceous plants, 'to put the garden to bed for winter', removes habitat, removes

It is important to have a clear plan and purpose in mind prior to pruning.

seed as a food source and prevents the enjoyment derived from observing frost on seed heads. Pruning fruiting and berrying shrubs as they finish flowering allows the flowers to provide pollen and nectar. By observing the fading flower heads, and minimising their removal, it is possible to make pruning decisions that both fulfil the pruning aims, while ensuring optimum berry production. This technique is particularly applicable to wall shrubs, for example, *Pyracantha* sp..

Many wall shrubs grow to the perfect height for nesting or roosting. Pruning of these shrubs and hedging plants should cease when the first signs of nesting behaviour are spotted, and only resumed in late summer when it has been ascertained that the last of the fledglings have flown the nest. If hedge pruning is then scheduled for October, which is a favoured month in many gardens, this results in the removal of berries, which are important food sources for wild birds and small mammals during the winter months. It would, therefore, be more beneficial to wildlife to prune in late winter when the berries have been eaten, rather than by a date scheduled in the diary.

Dead seed-heads add charm to the late summer garden, and can then get chopped and dropped.

Always prune outside the nesting season. Always check for ground- and low-nesting birds, like the robin, which nests in log piles or in tree trunks.

The seeds produced by plants are important food sources for birds and small mammals.

Pruning *Pyracantha* when flowering, allows unwanted growth to be pruned, with flowers left to form berries.

You Can't Stick It Back On!

Often when pruning, the focus is on the removal of growth. It is perhaps more important to focus and prioritise on what is being left. Key considerations could include:

- Ensuring that the plant is balanced.
- Maintaining a natural, rather than pruned, appearance.
- Leaving dead wood if colonised by moss or lichen.
- Provision of sufficient cover for wildlife.
- Ensuring sufficient depth to attract nesting wild birds.

Pruning to Create Habitat

This aspect of pruning is often overlooked. The application of a number of basic principles will ensure that the pruning creates habitats to welcome wildlife into the garden, while still ensuring aesthetics are maintained. A key consideration is the creation of ideal light levels for lower layers of planting. Adequate light levels can allow a wider range of plants to be cultivated, to add aesthetic interest and provide food and cover for wildlife. Plants such as the early flowering *Lamprocapnos spectabilis* (bleeding heart) require light-dappled shade, as do many of the smaller Japanese maples or the deliciously scented *Daphne bholua* 'Jacqueline Postill'. Careful pruning of trees and shrubs can create perfect positions for these plants.

Coppicing of plantings of *Corylus avellana* (hazel) also creates habitats for a wide range of spring flowers and wildlife. Even a small number of hazels can be divided into groups, which are cut on rotation, providing a totally renewable supply of bean poles and plant supports — a much more sustainable alternative than canes or any other product that has to be bought in. Coppicing prevents over-shading from the ever-developing canopies of trees, allowing light and air into the coppice. Even the smallest coppices can be home to a number of wildlife species, including dormice, *Hyacinthoides non-scripta* (bluebell) and *Primula vulgaris* (wild primrose).

Willow can also be pruned back to the ground to create a similar environment, but the withies so produced can be put to good use, with *Salix triandra* being prized for its supple qualities and used in basketry, while *Salix purpurea* is a popular choice for willow

That moment when your garden-harvested poles start to grow. (Spotted at RHS Garden Wisley.)

weaving. Willow weaving can create living arches, while planting willow withies can create charming living fences or hedges.

The watershoots that arise after hard pruning apple trees can be removed to produce smaller sticks ideal for growing peas in the productive garden, and so reduce the use of plastic netting.

Wrong Plant, Wrong Place

However effective one is with regard to pruning, the wrong plant in the wrong place will always be problematic. It is best practice to resolve such issues as soon as they are identified, rather than wait for the issue to escalate. One often sees houses with trees

The willow arch at Rosemary Cottage, Hook, East Yorkshire, which is open under the National Gardens Scheme.

Right plant, wrong place. This tree has been planted too close to the brick wall. Pruning cannot rectify poor planting decisions.

Did this tree so annoy the garden owner that all its branches had to be removed in punishment?

pressed up against the windows, blocking the entry of almost all light, or one sees trees starting to push walls over or, even worse, trees that must have so annoyed the garden owner that all their branches have been removed, as if in punishment.

It would be more appropriate for these plants to be removed and possibly recycled into log piles or hibernacula, replacing them with more appropriate plant species for the site.

Water Cups and Wet Crotches

Trees often have areas where water naturally collects. These water cups or wet crotches in trees provide a water supply to wildlife visiting the garden. This phenomenon can often be seen in teasels. Indeed, the gardens of apothecaries would be planted with such plants, as these were the only places where pure and unadulterated rainwater could be collected to use in tinctures and treatments.

Hedges

The management of garden hedges has a significant impact on their value as wildlife habitats. A mixed species' hedge allows wildlife to travel: bumblebees, birds, bats and butterflies all tend to travel along hedgerows, rather than venture across fields or open spaces. Generally, the evidence suggests that more relaxed hedge-cutting regimes result in a higher range of habitats. A report published by the Centre for Ecology and Hydrology reported that cutting hedges with hawthorn and blackthorn every three years, rather than on an annual cycle, more than doubled flowering. This increased flowering was also reported to result in an increase in the number and activity of pollinating insects, a greater yield of berries and an increase in both butterfly and moth caterpillars and pupae. Other research has shown that close-cut hedging supports fewer bird species and decreases the life-expectancy of the hedge. The reduction of bird species is significant, as approximately thirty-five species of wild birds nest in hedges, with fifty-five species visiting hedges to forage, nest or roost. The ecological benefit of the hedge is, of course, also dependent on the species of plants that make up the hedge. A privet hedge trimmed three or four times a year offers significantly fewer ecological benefits, compared to a wilder, mixed species' hedge that is cut every three years.

Hedge prunings can be used to create rustic, sustainable plant supports for perennials.

The Wildlife Trusts advise that hedges should be trimmed to an A-shape or profile. The thicker base of the hedge provides maximum protection for wildlife. The biodiversity of a hedge is also greatly increased by allowing buffer strips of unmown grass to grow under the hedge and at least 2m out from the base. This long grass, which can be planted with a range of wildflower species, provides an ideal environment for a wide range of birds, invertebrates and small mammals.

The height of the hedge can also influence the species of wild birds that will nest, with, for example, yellow hammers preferring hedges under 2m in height, while bullfinches and song thrushes are attracted to higher hedges or shrubs of around 4m.

There is also evidence that cutting a hedge to the same size every year, or rather cutting to the same point in the wood each year, can impact on plant health with a build-up of callus. It is better to allow a hedge to grow slightly larger each year or to vary the point of cutting, if this is appropriate to both species and garden style.

While considering the management of hedges it is also important to think about the selection of tools. The concept of human-powered, corded, battery, then hydrocarbon-powered tools as a last resort, discussed in Chapter 6, is equally applicable in this area of work.

Technique

While we have advocated a nuanced approach to pruning and the cutting of hedges, there are, however, some guiding principles:

- All equipment used should be well maintained and sharp. Secateurs and shears can be classed as

Japanese pruning saws offer exceptional cutting and replaceable blades. They cannot be sharpened by the gardener.

sharp if they can cleanly cut a thin sheet of paper. Blunt tools require more force, which can lead to accidents. Blunt tools also crush and damage plant stems; this damage results in slower healing and increases the surface area for fungal spores, and so increases the risk of disease.

- All equipment used should be sterile. We often use secateurs to cut out diseased wood. It is, therefore, good practice to use a sterilant to prevent the spread of disease. Proprietary products include Propellar, while some organisations prefer to use malt vinegar as a sterilant.
- If the branch is too wide for secateurs and loppers, then a sharp pruning saw should be used to prevent damage to tools.
- 'Never leave anything you can hang your coat on' — small stubs left through incorrect positioning of pruning cuts will die back and can infect the whole branch. Never leave stubs, always cutting back to a bud.
- Give the plant a clue as to how you want it to respond to the pruning intervention. If the aim is to create a plant with a formal goblet shape, and no branches crossing over within the plant, for example in the cultivation of gooseberries, then prune to an outward facing bud. Inward facing buds will produce unwanted branches that grow into the plant. Downward facing buds produce downward growth.
- If the plant to be pruned, for example an apple tree, has both vegetative buds and flower buds, learning how to identify the differences is important to ensure that flowering wood is not accidently removed.
- Ascertain if the plant flowers on the current year's growth, where hard pruning will produce strong, new growth to flower; or on older wood, where hard pruning removes the flowers for next year.

Training and Support Structures

Plants are often trained against walls using support wires or trellis. These support structures are permanent and so should be made from the highest quality materials that the budget will allow. The green plastic-coated wire used in many gardens is often short-lived and is not suited for use in sustainable gardens. Wire that is purchased from a chandler, which is designed to survive salt-laden water, will, in many cases, outlive the gardener and so is a more sustainable, 'buy once and buy good' alternative.

Off-the-shelf trellis structures are often poorly manufactured, with low-grade wood used that is often stapled rather than screwed. It is often problematic to ascertain if the wood used is certified as being from sustainably managed plantations. These trellis structures are difficult to treat and preserve with environment-friendly products, when clothed with plants. If the budget allows, a more sustainable option could be to procure local, artisan-made trellis, manufactured with FSC certified timber.

Record, Reflect, Repeat

We have used a lens of sustainability to consider pruning to enhance plant health, and to optimise and enhance the role that plants can offer to wildlife and biodiversity.

Recording, reflecting and repeating is an important discipline. This involves making notes and taking countless photographs, to record issues, work carried out and principle objectives achieved. Perhaps the aim is to alter hedge management to welcome song thrushes into the garden. The actions derived from this aim were to allow a section of planting to reach 4m. Has this worked? Have the song thrushes arrived? If so, all is good. If not, rethink, research and reflect to identify any other actions that might be required to achieve the objective.

Did the pruning technique reduce or increase flowering? Has the dead wood resulted in new and interesting lichen species or new fungi?

Top Tip

Compile a species' list for the garden, to record all the wildlife that interacts with the garden.

An annual species' list can give important feedback on the impacts of our gardening activities, and how these can impact on wildlife populations.

A green shield bug nymph, which is native to the British Isles. While it does feed on sap, it is considered to be part of the biodiversity present in a sustainable garden.

Top Tip

Keep secateurs and other cutting tools clean and sterile.

  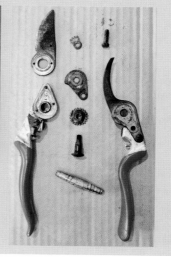

To avoid using harsh chemicals, secateurs can be dismantled and placed in a bath of tomato ketchup overnight. The acids in the ketchup work on the grime, which can then be washed or wiped away; a quick sharpen and the secateurs are good to go.

CHAPTER 8

COMPOSTS AND GROWING MEDIA

Look deep into nature and you will understand everything better.

Albert Einstein

This chapter investigates various aspects of the process of composting green waste. It looks at how the process can be made more sustainable. It considers the new and evolving area of compost teas. Finally, it looks at sustainable growing media for container growing.

Sustainable Composting

In previous chapters, this book has discussed the importance of reducing inputs. This action can include the generation of electricity, reduced water usage, the cultivation of home-grown mulch, the coppicing of hazel to produce beanpoles and eliminating synthetic fertilizers from our gardens. Every input that is avoided is a small step on the long road to sustainability, illustrating the concept that a sustainability journey is made up of a million tiny changes.

Equally important to reducing inputs is the reduction of waste from gardens. Every skip that leaves a new-build garden, and every bin filled with garden waste for kerbside collection, is an opportunity to be more sustainable that is being lost.

Sustainable composting offers the ultimate sustainable solution, and applies the concept of a circular economy, where plants grow, waste is produced, the waste is recycled and turned into a valuable product, which enhances the growth of plants and the development of soil within the garden. The sustainable gardener who is deep mulching their beds and using the 'no dig' or minimal cultivation techniques advocated and evaluated in Chapter 9, requires a plentiful supply of composted garden waste. While it can be argued that off-site composting is a lot less work, and so preferable, such an approach involves the use of fossil fuels in the transportation and the composting process, and results in a product that, due to the high temperatures involved in the process of composting, often has a lower population of microorganisms than on-site composting. The composted green waste that is the output of this process is, however, still a valuable resource. It can be blended (inoculated) with on-site compost to create a more beneficial product prior to use. It should be added that there is a concern that while the composted green waste is screened to remove sharp and foreign objects, there is an identified risk of introducing micro-plastics into the garden.

Even the smallest garden can, and should, have a compost heap. Compost heaps can be attractive and if one goes for a beehive-style compost heap, or a more traditional wooden structure, they can blend into the character and style of the garden. From a sustainability perspective, the positioning and the construction of compost heaps should be carefully considered. A variety of composting solutions could be considered. Insulated and ventilated hot-composting systems are efficient and effective; however, like off-site composting, they can produce a relatively sterile product. They do, however, allow us to compost weeds that have gone to seed, diseased plant material and perennial weeds, as the high temperatures will break these materials down. While these composting systems are often manufactured using plastics, they are highly effective and last for a great many years. There are other compost bins made of plastics that are more problematic. The thinner plastic bins offer few identifiable advantages over other materials. Plastic offers very low insulation properties; it does not keep heaps warm during colder months. These bins often have no ventilation. This limits the movement of air into the bin. This in turn limits the population of microorganisms, whose role is to break down the plant material, thus producing compost. These types of composting bin are neither effective nor sustainable.

Wood is an excellent material for constructing compost bins. It has a high insulation value, is easy to work with, allowing bins to be constructed with ease. When building compost bins out of wood, our usual checks should be made from a sustainability perspective. Is the wood produced to a high environmental standard? Is it certified, ideally to a standard such as Forest Stewardship Council (FSC)? Was it grown locally to reduce the carbon footprint involved in transport? We often use reclaimed or repurposed wood when building compost bins, with pallets being a favourite choice of many gardeners. As discussed in Chapter 5, caution should be exercised when using pallets. There is a risk of introducing plant pests, especially wood-boring larvae, when working with untreated pallet wood.

Once a supply of suitable timber has been secured, our next decision is how we treat the timber. While one can purchase carbon-positive paint products, paints can be damaging to the environment in a number of ways. Many of the raw materials in paint are derived from fossil fuels or involve considerable inputs of energy in their manufacture. Solvent-based paints and wood preservatives contain volatile organic compounds (VOCs), which contribute to air pollution. Paint is often supplied in single-use plastic containers or tins, and while there are take-back schemes operated by some companies, many of these containers end up in landfill. Other issues to consider are the potential impacts of cleaning brushes, adding micro-contaminations to water. There is also the potential of any preservative or chemical contained within paint leaching into the compost being produced. The negative impacts of paints and preservatives need to be carefully considered against the potential advantage of an increased lifespan of the timber.

The siting of the compost heap is another important consideration. While this is often an aesthetic-based decision, there are practical reasons why a shaded position is more favourable. A shaded position helps to reduce the drying of the material being composted. This reduces the need to add water to maintain the composting process. The compost heap should also be positioned away from water sources, as any leachate produced could cause eutrophication of water sources.

The planning of the composting process is an important consideration. Advocates of no-dig systems often suggest a 20cm top dressing of garden compost on an annual basis. Calculating the volume of composted garden waste required to meet the needs of the garden on an annual basis would inform the construction of appropriately sized composting bins to be undertaken, if space allows. To prevent the requirement of buying in composted green waste, it may be necessary when considering planting to devote a small area of the garden to the production of bulky plant material, such as *Miscanthus* or willow, which can be shredded and composted to meet the needs of the garden.

The compost heap is often a home to wildlife and while keeping the area around the compost heap clear and positioning the compost heap to be away from a fence can reduce the incidence of vermin-dwelling in the heap, I have been delighted to welcome (after the initial surprise!) a small family of field mice into my own bin, along with large numbers of woodlice, whose role is to pass the organic material through their bodies as part of the composting process. Other gardeners have been lucky enough to find slowworms in their heaps. The process of gardening to increase biodiversity often results in unexpected guests. These guests should be treasured and welcomed, and added to our list of wildlife that the garden is benefiting, rather than feared.

Compost heaps are often made out of pallet wood. Care should be taken from a biosecurity perspective that this does not import pests into the garden (see Chapter 5).

Compost heaps can be made with no structure to bound the sides. This example at Great Dixter also appeared to be a hibernaculum.

Plastic compost bins come in a variety of designs. The lack of ventilation (to allow oxygen to diffuse into the heap to meet the needs of microorganisms) often limits their effectiveness.

Wood makes an excellent material for compost heap design, as it keeps the heap insulated over the winter.

Compost heaps benefit from a roof, which prevents rain, especially in the winter, from cooling the heap, so slowing the composting process.

Finally, many gardens use shredders when preparing material for composting. When run on renewable electricity these offer few issues from a sustainability perspective, if they are already being used. However, we should also remember our mantra that human-powered is best when considering replacement. Old, hand-cranked silage or root choppers make excellent shredders and can often be found at farm sales. Otherwise, simply using pruning shears and secateurs can result in excellent compost production.

Compost Teas

The use of garden composts as soil improvers is well established. They provide a food source for soil micro-organisms, which consume and further break down this material, resulting in a build-up of humic products within the soil. The addition of garden compost, as a soil improver, boosts the number of macro- and microorganisms within the soil. This is in part due to the presence of microorganisms within the compost; but also, because compost is a food source for these organisms.

There is an argument, which is open to debate, that it would be beneficial to produce (brew) a product that contains a high population of these beneficial microorganisms. This product could be added to the soil, especially one that is low in populations of micro-organisms, to inoculate it and to aid the production of humic products. Advocates of this school of thinking brew a compost tea to contain maximum numbers of microorganisms and apply these to the soil as a drench. If there is sufficient organic material in the soil to allow these microorganisms to survive (organic matter being the food source for these organisms), then this process can be beneficial. There are risks that the addition of certain species may upset the ecological balance of soil microorganisms, and residues of sugar or molasses used in the production of the compost teas can cause the scorching of the young roots of germinating seedlings. Other concerns relating to this practice include the potential for the tea to contain *Escherichia coli* or other dangerous pathogens.

There is little, if any, conclusive evidence to indicate that this is a beneficial practice; however, the concept is currently trending and research studies continue to be undertaken to identify if there are any identifiable advantages. Those wishing to trial this technique are directed to the Permaculture website where there is further information (please *see* 'Further Resources' for further details).

The Importance of Microbiota

If one leaves multiple slices of bread in the open air, they will all go mouldy as a result of fungal spores contained in the air. If, however, one looks at plants growing in a late summer garden, some will have disease on them and some will be healthy. This leads to the question, if every slice of bread goes mouldy because of spores in the air, then why do all the leaves of a susceptible plant species not get attacked with fungi? On investigation there are multiple factors at play. One could argue that the health status of the plant has a significant impact. The relative thickness of the cuticle could also play an impact. There is, however, a concept that colonies of microorganisms live on the leaves of the plant. These microorganisms help to provide protection from airborne disease, much in the same way that a diverse range of microorganisms in our guts protect us.

The concept that leaves host diverse communities of microbes is known as microbiota. It is thought that these communities offer the plant a range of benefits. Chapter 3 discussed the benefits that bacteria offer plants in the rhizosphere. In the aerial parts of the plant, these benefits are thought to revolve around the prevention of fungal disease. Chapter 5 discussed the role of biostimulants on plant health. There is some evidence that the microorganisms present on the leaf may provide an antagonism, improving the health status of the plant.

The compost teas previously discussed are rich in microorganisms and there is a growing body of evidence to suggest that when these are sprayed on to the leaves of plants, the microbiota is strengthened. Compost tea systems, such as System 10 from Growing Solutions allow gardens to test this concept. Some commercial growers use compost teas as part of their Nursery Health Plans to boost the plants' ability to combat diseases. It should be noted that this is a new and novel area of horticulture and so the results of academic, peer-reviewed studies are required before this practice can be advocated with certainty.

Growing Media

The sale of growing media within domestic gardens is driven by the appeal and the availability of containers, along with the rising number of people renting properties, where planting into the soil is undesirable. While container gardening offers the opportunity to grow a wider range of plant material, including species that are not suited to local soil conditions, it offers many challenges from a sustainability perspective.

The reuse of existing pots comes with a considerably lower environmental impact, and a wide range of items can be repurposed to become planters. However, many of these containers at end of life are unlikely to be recycled. Virgin pots are more problematic, even those using recycled plastics in their manufacture are unlikely themselves to be recycled. Those made from terracotta or metal use raw materials that require extraction from the earth and are processed using high-energy, intensive processes. They are often made overseas. A report on the employment conditions of the staff involved in their production is not always available to the purchaser. These products are often shipped in containers many thousands of miles to reach retailers and distributers. The plants growing within these containers are more likely to be short-term plants that have a higher environmental footprint and will require the application of feeds, the production of which directly impacts on climate change.

A delivery of Westland's 'Jack's Magic' growing media at a garden centre. This is a 50 per cent peat-based growing medium. An estimated 50,000 articulated lorry loads of growing media are used in horticulture each year.

The final consideration is the growing medium itself. In the UK, it is estimated that we use in the region of 50,000 articulated lorry loads of what is predominantly a peat-based product every year. The Horticultural Trades Association reports that the UK uses over 3 million cubic metres of growing media every year. It is the volume of growing media used that is problematic.

The UK Government is banning the sale of peat to amateur gardeners in 2024, and in professional growing by 2028.

Peat is an excellent growing medium and has been used in horticulture for many years. It is water-retentive, free-draining, uniform, can pass through automated machinery with few problems and is sterile. If it were not for the environmental devastation caused by its use, it would be a perfect substrate for growing.

The key arguments related to the banning of peat as a growing medium include:

- The Joint Nature Conservation Committee (JNCC) report that the UK has lost 94 per cent of its lowland peatlands.
- The International Union for the Conservation of Nature (IUCN) report that 80 per cent of all UK peatlands are damaged.
- UK peatlands store 3 billion tonnes of carbon.
- UK peatlands store more carbon than all the forests in the UK, France and Germany.
- In England, only 4 per cent of upland, deep peatlands are in good condition.
- The United Nations Environmental Programme has reported that, while peatlands only account for 3 per cent of the earth's surface, they contain 30 per cent of the total soil carbon, and contain more than twice the amount of carbon stored in the world's forest.
- When peatlands are drained, or peat is extracted for use in growing, it breaks down, releasing this stored carbon as a greenhouse gas.
- The peat that is valued in growing media forms at a rate of 1mm per year.
- Peat provides valuable services, for example the filtration of water, which reduces the treatment required from water companies.
- The drainage of peatlands and associated agricultural use, have led to peatlands being amongst the highest sources of greenhouse gas emissions in the UK.

- Peat bogs offer a unique habitat and are biodiverse spaces. Peat extraction removes habitat for rare birds, butterflies, dragonflies and plants.
- The usage of peat emits 400,000 tonnes of carbon each year.
- Lord Nicholas Stern, author of the Stern Review and an advisor on climate change, estimates that every tonne of carbon released has a future cost of £150 to mediate for climate change.

Rethinking Growing Media

There are a number of alternative products that can be used to replace peat in growing media, but each of these has its advantages and its limitations.

Coir

Coir is a by-product of the coconut industry and is, essentially, the ground husks and dust of the hairy casing

Peat-free growing media offers significant environmental advantages. Cultivation techniques should be matched to the characteristics of the main bulk ingredients.

of the coconut. It is widely used in the formulation of peat-free growing media. The coconut fibre can be ground to differing sizes giving a material suitable for use in module trays through to potting-on.

Coir offers many advantages: it provides a good level of air-filled porosity to the growing media (depending on the milling); it is relatively slow to decompose and so prevents the air-filled porosity reducing over time; it is horticulturally sterile and free of weeds; it has a pH of 5.5–6.8, depending on the source and so does not require lime to correct the acidity, as peat does. Coir is from a renewable resource and it is suggested that the lignin content of the coir benefits bacterial growth in the media. It is able to hold water very well. It often looks dry on the surface of the growing medium, while being damp below the surface. This can result in overwatering, which is a main reason why plants fail in coir-based composts. It has a high cation-exchange capacity, which means it is very good at holding on to nutrient salts and preventing them from leaching out of the growing media.

Limitations with regard to the use of coir include the use of water in the production process, which has a major impact on sustainability, especially as water is often in short supply in the regions where coir is produced. The transportation of coir is also problematic, as this result in carbon emissions.

Composted Bark/Forest Residue

This product, which can be ground to different grades, can be used as a bulk ingredient in growing media. Depending on the grade, it can improve air-filled porosity and water-holding capacity. It is often produced from brash, or forest residue, often from UK woodlands. Composted bark is often added to growing media, with 20 per cent by volume added to seed and cutting mixes and up to 50 per cent to potting mixes. There is some evidence that adding composted bulk ingredients to growing media can introduce very low levels of pathogen to the growing media. The levels are not high enough to cause plant health risks but do trigger a response within the plant that can make it less susceptible to pathogen attack when planted out in the soil.

Limitations include the fact that not all composted bark is from FSC managed woodlands and even those brands that mention FSC often report on a percentage FSC bark, for example 50 per cent. Some barks contain allelopathic chemicals. These are chemicals released by plant roots to control the growth of neighbouring plants. Bark can contain chemicals that inhibit germination of certain weed seeds. Bark made from these species is best avoided when considering use in a seed mix. If the bark is not sufficiently composted, then the decomposition process can continue in use and deplete nitrogen levels in the growing media.

There are numerous other potential peat replacements, including wood pulps, which are widely used currently to reduce the percentage peat in peat-based mixes. Recycled urban waste can be used; however, this is a widely variable product, depending on the source of the green waste. The variability impacts on the uniformity of plants cultivated in it. Some producers use rice husks, which make an excellent growing medium with a high air-filled porosity; however, the supplies are limited, and so this material is not widely available. Other products, such as perlite and vermiculite, are problematic as the raw rock-based material requires shipping and high temperatures to produce the usable products.

Bracken

Bracken has been used as a soil improver by hill farmers for many years. It was traditionally cut and allowed to dry. The resulting product was used as animal bedding over winter and used to fertilise farmland after use. There is a growing interest in the harvesting, composting and use of the resulting material, which is rich in potassium, as a growing medium. Dalefoot Composts has pioneered the use of bracken in composts. This is an example of one of the new artisan-produced growing media, which have performed well in trials. There are still issues relating to sustainability, with regard to bagging in single-use plastics and transportation.

Sustainable Solutions

Rethinking the usage of growing media is the first stage in the process. A series of questions can be asked to inform decisions relating to growing media usage:

- Is it necessary to start these seedlings in pots?
- Could these seedlings be sown in the open ground?
- Could water be used as a propagation medium rather than growing media?
- Is it necessary to plant into containers?
- Could these plants be grown in the open ground?
- Could a paving slab be lifted to allow planting into the soil?
- Would changing from cultivating short-term plants to perennials be acceptable?
- Could growing media be refreshed and reused in containers?

Trees are sometimes planted in containers rather than the open ground, in new housing developments.

The concept that growing media can be refreshed and reused is problematic to many horticulturists as it is a reversal of previous best practice, which was to always use fresh, growing media when refilling containers to reduce the risk of pests, especially vine weevil.

When one rethinks these principles, and considers strategies to reduce and reuse, this concept is worthy of further thought. The key risks can be identified, and then mitigations considered. Risks to plant health could be reduced by ensuring that any growing media that is to be reused is restricted to being sourced from containers that have shown no plant health issues, for example there have been no signs of vine weevil attack within the root zone or notched edges to leaves. The collected growing media can be broken up with major roots removed. Prior to reuse, it can be refreshed by having a proportion of new growing media added to it,

A young plant showing excellent root growth in a refreshed, peat-free growing medium.

and a small quantity of base dressing of natural, organic, slow-release fertilizer mixed into it. Gardeners would be advised to evaluate the performance of this refreshed growing media compared to virgin growing media.

Other options available to gardens include the manufacture of growing media made from composted materials. The International Union for the Conservation of Nature (IUCN), in their publication *Peat-free Horticulture, Demonstrating Success* suggests garden-made composts as a viable alternative to purchased media.

Suggestions include a seed-sowing mix made from finely sieved garden soil, horticultural sand and leaf mould. The soil element for this mix would benefit from heat sterilisation to kill weed seeds; this could be achieved by placing the sieved soil in a baking tin or tray and laying this on the embers of a fire pit.

Swedish plantsman and designer Peter Korn suggests a growing medium produced by mixing one part garden compost to three parts horticultural sand. Another mix is produced by combining 80 per cent pumice, 10 per cent horticultural sand and 10 per cent sustainably produced biochar.

The IUCN report also observes that many perennials can be divided and placed straight into their planting positions, eliminating the potting process and growing media altogether.

Local Growing Media for Local People

While the growing media market is dominated by a few larger companies, the transportation of a heavy bulky material from one end of the country to another is hard to justify, however sustainable the bulk ingredients might be. As the growing media market changes and evolves, there are local companies starting to offer an artisan-made, local growing medium that is made from local, natural materials. As well as supporting the local economy and providing jobs for local people, the resulting growing medium can be supplied with a low carbon footprint.

Did you know?

A 10m deep peat bed takes 9,000 years to form. As a result, peat preserves a record of past vegetation, landscapes, and people. However, in 2011 90% of the peat bogs in the UK had been lost, taking with them history, rare plants and wildlife.

Many organizations are moving to selling plants produced in peat-free growing media, including the National Trust, who are also looking at the supply chain for fresh produce sold in their cafés, to reduce peat usage in, for example, mushroom and cress production.

PRODUCTIVE GROWING

If we do not get our cities, homes, and gardens in order, so that they feed and shelter us, we must lay waste to all other natural systems. Thus, truly responsible conservationists have gardens....

Bill Mollison (the father of permaculture)

One of the most significant ways that most people can reduce their carbon footprint is in the production of their own fruit, vegetables and herbs. Food production releases 37 per cent of all global greenhouse gas emissions. While our diets can have a significant impact on this figure (with plant-based diets producing half the emissions of animal-based diets), the greatest impact of all comes from the simple act of growing our own food.

The benefits of productive growing are, however, not limited to carbon footprints. Studies have shown that the very act of growing our own food has measurable impacts on our health and wellness.

While traditional growing systems require considerable inputs in terms of water, fertilizer and often plastic products, there are numerous growing systems that embrace the core principles of sustainability.

Forest Gardens

The basic concept behind forest gardening is to create productive growing ecosystems. Forest gardens are based on a set of over-riding principles, which include many of the concepts discussed in preceding chapters: embracing biodiversity, observing and recording, practising minimal interventions, using resources with care and connecting with others.

Many forest gardens are built on the principles of layers, which replicate those seen in nature. Ideally, each layer is made up of productive plants. Upper canopy plants would be taller trees that could produce edible nuts amongst their ecosystem services, such as *Castanea sativa* (sweet chestnut). The sub-canopy might include more traditional fruit trees, such as apple, plum or cherry. The next layer might be comprised of climbers that provide edible fruits, such as vines or runner beans. The shrub layer could be comprised of fruit bushes, such as gooseberry or redcurrant, with herbaceous plants such as Jerusalem artichoke, rhubarb or herbs making up the next layer. The ground layer could include plants such as strawberries, winter squash or wild garlic. The final layer is of root crops, such as horseradish, beetroots, turnips, onions and carrots.

Purists will note that some of the suggested crops are not perennial and might argue that they do not belong in a forest garden as they require a greater intervention. It is widely acknowledged, however, that the term forest garden is a fluid one, with some advocating the seven-layer approach suggested here, while others advocate a three-layer approach.

Wineberry. Suitable for herbaceous/ground-layer plantings.

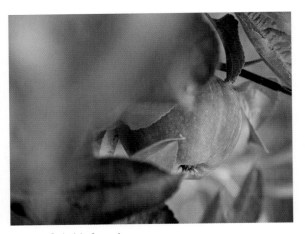

Apples. Suitable for sub-canopy.

Raspberry. Suitable for the climber layer.

Redcurrants. Suitable for shrub-layer plantings.

Whichever model is used, forest gardens can be defined by the following over-riding principles:

- Minimal inputs.
- Minimal interventions.
- Perennial crops.
- Being functioning ecosystems.

Benefits include the concept that forest gardens can lock up more carbon than traditional growing methods and allow a stronger soil-based ecosystem to develop.

Permaculture

Permaculture has three key principles: looking after the Earth, taking care of all of its people and dividing resources equally, including giving back to the Earth. The principles of permaculture can be applied to many aspects of life, rather than just productive growing. Planting trees for shade, using dead wood to create habitats or produce food, the harvesting of rainwater and reduced use of inputs are all consistent with this philosophy. The cultivation of soil is discouraged as this can impact on its unseen ecosystem. Permaculture seeks to mimic nature, rather than try to control it, and so plant pests are viewed as part of biodiversity and the food chain. Herbicides and synthetic fertilizers are inconsistent to this approach and so are not used.

Permaculture and forest gardening share many core principles. Indeed, forest gardening is often seen as part of the permaculture movement. A fundamental difference in permaculture is greater freedom to cultivate annual crops, biennial crops and the growing of tuberous plants. Some would argue that this approach is more suited to those who garden in a temperate climate; however, there are many compelling examples of permaculture gardens in the UK.

Organics

The principles of organic production were discussed in Chapter 1. The organic movement promotes the development of soil health and fertility, which naturally results in increased biodiversity and reduced inputs. Many of the core concepts of organic production from the prohibition of synthetic pesticides and synthetic fertilizers to the restrictions on the use of other environmentally damaging inputs are to be welcomed. The sustainable gardener could take these important core concepts and question further some of the interventions that are allowed within organic growing systems, for example the use of natural pesticides, such as pyrethrum, which are not specific, and target a wide spectrum of both pests and beneficial organisms. Organic growers can cultivate soil-releasing carbon, can apply animal manures and natural fertilizers, and use large volumes of water and fossil fuels. The sustainable gardener would build on the principles of organic growing and seek to enhance them.

Six Principles of Productive Growing

1. Planning

This is one of the most important aspects to both traditional and sustainable productive growing. Planning starts with the design and the layout of the space available. Productive gardens can be designed as potagers. These productive spaces are often defined as being informal or romantic. They would suit country gardens and are closely related to a traditional cottage garden. (However, while the cottage garden is centred around flowers and decorative plants, the potager is centred around vegetables.)

A more utilitarian option may be to lay out the available land into a series of beds, of productive units. Beds offer significant advantages: they allow access to

Tendrils are not just functional, they add aesthetic value to plantings.

Salad leaves catching the early summer sun.

The male sweetcorn flower, releasing pollen.

The silk tassels of sweetcorn, ready to catch airborne pollen.

Tomato flowers have a unique charm and beauty when you get up close.

'The past is a foreign country, they do things differently there' (L. P. Hartley). Single and double digging are no longer best practice in productive growing.

the site without the need to stand on soil and they work particularly well with no-dig gardening. The key concept of the no-dig system is that soil cultivation is replaced with the application of deep mulches made from composted garden waste. Proponents often specify a mulching depth of 20cm. A wooden frame or shuttering is used while adding the composted garden waste to the bed, but removed after the mulch has been allowed to settle. (This removes a habitat for slugs between the soil and the timber and reduces the quantity of timber required.)

Key advantages of the no-dig system are:

- Organic matter is broken down to humic compounds faster on the surface of the soil than when incorporated.
- The humic compounds promote the aggregation of soil particles into soil crumbs.
- The presence of a developing crumb structure that is not damaged by cultivation improves the diffusion of oxygen into the soil and improves drainage.
- The improved crumb structure of the soil results in a higher water-holding capacity, with more water being made available to plants.
- The increase in organic matter contained in the soil sequesters carbon.
- The plentiful supply of organic matter provides a food source for microorganisms, which enhance the soil ecology.

- The lack of cultivation and the deep mulching reduces the incidence of annual weed (assuming the mulch is relatively free of weed seeds, e.g. from hot composting).
- The reduced cultivation favours the development of stronger mycorrhizal relationships.
- There is strong evidence that yields are increased, in particular on poor soils.

It should be noted that while there is strong evidence, supported by the results of field trials, there is a lack of peer-reviewed evidence relating to no dig. The publication of formal papers would be welcomed.

Square foot gardening is an ideal system for smaller spaces. Using this system, growing areas can be divided up into 1 square foot growing units. These growing spaces can be included in potagers, in no-dig beds and traditional growing systems. The key concept is to cultivate each square as an individual unit; perhaps planting four lettuces in one unit and fifteen radish or carrots in the next unit. When one square is harvested, it is planted up with further crops. Most crops can be grown using this system, with climbing plants being produced towards the back of a bed. Some crops, such as potatoes, sweetcorn and trailing marrow, are not suitable for square foot gardening.

An advantage of both potagers and square foot gardens is the opportunity to practise companion planting or mixed cropping. As discussed in Chapter 5, studies have shown that pests often require the presence of significant quantities of crop plants to trigger egg-laying. The reduced areas of monocropping in these systems act to deter egg-laying. Square foot gardens have shown themselves to offer significant increases in yield over conventional productive growing systems.

Gantt charts can be used to plan sowing, planting, harvesting and replanting to maximise the full potential of productive areas, and ensure twelve-month cropping and year-round soil cover. Apps are also available to allow further maximisation of space.

2. Propagation

Propagation is a major element of productive growing, especially when one considers concepts such as weekly or fortnightly seed sowing to ensure continuity of supply to avoid gluts and wastage of food. Propagation is also an area where radical rethinking can dramatically reduce the environmental impact of our gardening.

Crops are often started in pots or seed trays. This method of starting productive crops is problematic and arguably wasteful of resources. Even when using plastic-free pots or reusing yogurt or similar plastic containers, a growing medium is required. If the growing medium used is not sourced from the garden, then this results in the use of plastic packaging and transportation. Pots require significant inputs of water. Rethinking is required to reduce the environmental cost of propagating productive crops. While some tender productive crops require higher temperatures for germination or are better started in pots (such as courgettes and sweetcorn), many grow well when sown in situation (such as beetroot and spinach).

The direct sowing of seeds requires a suitable seed bed. Techniques can include the stale seedbed technique, where the ground is cultivated and a seedbed is prepared. This is then left to allow weeds to germinate (weed germination being triggered by exposure to light during cultivation). The weeds are then carefully removed with minimum soil disturbance and crops can be sown. If the soil is heavy and a fine tilth is difficult to achieve, then the no-dig concept of a deep mulch layer of garden compost would provide ideal germination conditions. If a little heat is required, then cloches can be used. Direct sowing into a suitable soil or mulch results in plants that grow away strongly and do not suffer from transplanting stress.

Where tender productive plants are to be propagated, pots should be reused and filled with a refreshed or reused growing medium, Seedlings have low-nutrient requirements and so a growing medium that is exhausted could be ideal from this perspective. The growing medium could be blended with a small proportion of virgin peat-free compost and the mix can then be sterilised. In domestic settings this could be achieved by adding the growing media mix to a large tin. This can then be placed in a cooling oven once foodstuffs have been removed or on the grid of a cooling BBQ, if handling growing medium in a kitchen does not appeal. This will achieve heat sterilisation of the growing medium mix. In professional settings, heat-sterilising units could be installed. Liquid feeds of dilute comfrey or nettle tea can be given after germination to support growth processes in the young plant.

The sourcing of seed is a critical aspect when propagating. Organically produced seed will have been grown without contamination by synthetic pesticides and will have been produced without inputs of synthetic fertilizers, which lowers the carbon footprint along with the other benefits of organic production. Organic seed will also have avoided seed dressings, which often contain synthetic pesticides or fungicides. These are problematic as they negatively impact on the soil, for example fungicides within a seed dressing will prevent the development of mycorrhizal relationships, which could otherwise benefit the plant. Seed should also be sourced from reliable sources. Some plant diseases are transmitted by seed and low-cost seed, from unknown sources, can end up with the introduction of plant pathogens. If seed is being imported or purchased from sources outside of the UK, then biosecurity should be a prime consideration

The high cost of seed, coupled with the desire to reuse and reduce waste, has led to concepts such as seed swaps, where gardeners come together and share surplus seeds. Seedysunday.org has recently celebrated twenty years of seed swapping. If there are no seed-swap events near to you, then they are very straightforward to start up.

Other considerations with regard to seed are the benefits in vigour of selecting F1 and F2 hybrids, along with the considerable benefits that can be derived from selecting resistant cultivars and recording the performance of different cultivars and crops within the garden.

Some seeds require a specific temperature to trigger germination, for example cucumbers, as a productive crop, require a temperature of 20°C. Electric propagators offer an effective tool to ensure optimum germination and are particularly appropriate for use in sustainable gardening when powered by renewable energy. Those with tunnels or larger greenhouses could use the heat generated from the composting process to both keep their growing spaces frost-free, while also providing bottom heat for germination. This technique is particularly useful for horticultural settings that are off-grid. A wooden framework, which could be constructed from woven willow sourced from the garden, is filled with shredded or finely chopped plant material, garden compost or manure. Natural activators, such as comfrey, can be added. A slatted wood top can then be laid over this heap. As the composting process occurs, heat is released. Seed trays can be laid

Resistance Is...

An allotment site that is infected with club root of cabbage could be considered unsuitable using the right plant, right place model of thinking.

An alternative strategy is to select cultivars such as Brussels sprout 'Crispus' F1, cabbage 'Kilaton' and cauliflower 'Clapton', which would allow cultivation of brassicas without the need for further interventions.

Garden Health Plan

A Garden Health Plan could also suggest strategies to support resistance within the cultivars suggested. This is particularly important for cultivars that only show partial resistance. Examples relating to club root include the elimination of weeds that can become infested with, and so harbour, club root, the growing of cabbages in small containers to avoid root damage on planting out and the planting out of larger, more resistant plants.

Recycling Myths

Many plants sold are now available in taupe pots, in PEP plastic trays or in containers made of recycled plastics.

The reality is that these containers require a considerable input of energy in manufacture. Contaminants, such as growing media residue, limit their recyclability and even when recycled, the process takes a considerable amount of energy. It is better, where it is possible, to wash, sterilise and reuse existing pots to reduce the plastic footprint of the garden.

- Globe artichokes.
- Nine-star broccoli.
- Perennial kales.
- Ransomes.
- Rhubarb.
- Tree onions.

It should also be remembered that top fruit and soft fruit are also grown as perennial crops.

3. Cultivation Practices

Cultivation practices make a huge difference on the environmental footprint of the productive growing space. Processes should be rethought, researched, with negative aspects reduced and results being recorded. For example, should the surface of the soil be cultivated with a hoe to remove spontaneous non-crop plants? Alternative strategies could include:

- Allowing a small number of non-crop plants to grow, to provide pollen, nectar and leaves for foraging caterpillars.
- Should the removal of spontaneous plants be limited to those that act as secondary hosts for pests and diseases?
- Should specific spontaneous plants be selected to encourage pollinators or beneficial insects into the garden, for example dandelions to encourage bumblebees?
- If the removal of spontaneous plants is required, should hoes be sharpened and the angle of the blade adjusted to allow for the severing of plant and root with minimal soil movement?

on the slatted wood to benefit from the bottom heat provided. This technique offers a carbon-neutral, totally natural source of heat that can be used to start and maintain a frost-free environment for the propagation of tender productive crops.

Many young vegetable plants are available to purchase from garden centres. They can be useful to 'top up' productive areas or offer the advantage of earlier planting times than can be achieved with home-grown plants. These plants are likely to have been grown in plastic containers, in peat-based composts and have had high water and fossil fuel inputs, as they are often produced in large, heated glasshouses.

Perennial vegetables are favoured by proponents of forest gardening and permaculture. They require minimum inputs, and are deserving of a place in productive gardens, regardless of the philosophy being followed. Care should be taken when planning the positioning of perennial crops, as by their nature they are permanent features of the garden.

Perennial vegetables include:

- Asparagus.
- Cardoons.

- Simple trials can be undertaken to ascertain if the presence of spontaneous plants has a negative impact on yield.
- Thresholds for action can be determined and recorded to inform maintenance strategies and schedules.

Action thresholds are an important concept in sustainable gardening. Previous chapters have considered the principle of minimal interventions. There is a fine line between carrying out frequent interventions (which may favour the specific plant being cultivated, but at significant environmental cost), with interventions that are delayed too long (resulting in a lack of control of the area). Balance is required between the two extremes, with trials and experimentation to identify the critical points of intervention. This concept was introduced in Chapter 6 when determining the ideal mowing regimes to benefit wildflowers within lawns.

Action thresholds should be identified when considering the range of plant health threats to productive crops. Slugs are often rightly considered to be pests; however, the RHS has recently reported that thirty-five of the forty-four species of slug in the UK do not feed on garden plants. They quietly go about their job of clearing our gardens from dead wood and similar dead organic matter. The nine species of slug that predate on plants are also part of the wider garden ecosystem. They are useful food sources for newts, frogs, toads, ducks and some species of wild birds. If slugs pose a problem and are damaging crops, then a Garden Health Plan can be developed to consider the full range of control measures. Reducing the conditions that favour slugs would be a first step; this can include improving general garden hygiene to remove such a habitat. It is worth noting that a single slug can lay as many as 500 eggs in a growing season, which could result in over 90,000 grandchildren every year. As gardens are not overrun with slugs to the magnitude that this statistic might suggest, it is reasonable to assume that they are controlled, in the main, by the garden ecosystem. Strengthening this ecosystem would, therefore, appear to be a wiser way of reducing populations rather than the sprinkling of pellets. Although these pellets now use iron phosphate as the active ingredient, they are still regarded as problematic from a sustainability perspective. They require manufacture, are supplied in single-use plastics and have an impact (albeit minor) on the garden ecosystem. It may be more appropriate to create a habitat that does not favour slugs but that does suit frogs and toads as agents of control.

Fruit crops, as permanent additions to productive gardens, can build up effective, beneficial relationships with soil bacteria and mycorrhiza. Fruit, therefore, does not normally require feeding in settings that have healthy soil ecosystems. Vegetable crops on the other hand, do often require the additional nutrition to maximise yields. Synthetic fertilizers have no place in a sustainable garden. Their manufacture, as previously stated, has a major impact on climate change. These feeds can also leach through the soil during periods of high rainfall (especially ones that are high in nitrates) and this can lead to eutrophication of waterways. Alternatives could include 'manufacturing' fertilizers from within the garden. Deep-rooted weeds, grass clippings and plant-based kitchen waste often have valuable nutrition within them and can be composted. Other techniques include making fertilizer teas. These are made by cutting nettles or comfrey, roughly chopping them and adding them to water to create a stock solution. Seaweed and other natural feeds are totally acceptable; however, they do involve plastics and emissions from transportation.

Other useful cultivation techniques involve the use of green manures. These are useful in protecting the surface from damage during major rain events. Leguminous green manures can also be used to add nitrogen to the soil. Autumn-sown white mustard is particularly recommended as a green manure, as it is killed by frost and so does not need to be incorporated and so is suitable for use in a no-dig bed.

4. Grow Your Own

This can be extended to the cultivation of our own crop supports, which is another area where rethinking is required. Many gardeners would consider bamboo canes to be natural and so sustainable. However, these are produced overseas on land that may be better used to feeding local people. They also require transportation and, while better than plastics, they are problematic. Prunings or poles harvested from the

The World Food Garden at RHS Garden Wisley showcases sustainable techniques, including the use of garden-grown crop supports, which add a rustic charm to the garden.

coppicing of hazel (if the garden is large enough) offer more self-sufficient, sustainable alternatives.

As previously suggested, it is possible to grow plants such as *Miscanthus* to provide organic material that can be used as a mulch.

It is a wise practice when planning any input for a garden to pause and rethink:

- Why is this product a necessary input?
- How could I produce this product within my own garden?
- Is this product really necessary?

5. Scouting

Scouting involves the close observation of crops. In the fruit garden, the early signs of brown rot on apple should be scouted and removed from the tree immediately to reduce the risk of spore release, which could result in the infection of other developing/ripening fruit. Plants are inspected regularly to check if they are ready for harvesting. Scouting (and recording findings) allows us to develop our knowledge of the garden. For example, often the first flowers abort on runner beans, with the cropping starting later in the season. When scouted and recorded, this gives reassurance in future years. Scouting also allows us to consider how well different cultivars are responding to the microclimates within our own gardens. As previously suggested, successful cultivars should be recorded to ensure that they are cultivated in future years. Pest-control strategies recorded build up vital information about the garden.

Regular scouting can reveal early infections of aphid, which can be controlled with blasts of water if numbers climb above the treatment threshold.

6. Harvesting

Harvesting is the culmination of much hard work. Gluts when crops come together can result in food wastage and so recording should be used. Have the crops given the required continuity of supply, or should sowing dates be rethought and amended for the next season?

Surplus crops can obviously be given to friends and family, blanched and frozen, or turned into jams, chutneys and pickles. Food banks will sometimes be prepared to take and share fresh produce. This simple action can help to tackle (albeit in a very small way) deprivation and food inequality. Some local community groups collect surplus high-quality fruit and vegetables from allotments and other gardens to create manageable deliveries for participating food banks.

Folklore suggests that it is only possible to think happy thoughts when eating a tomato warmed by the summer sun. Fresh produce boost wellness and reduces food miles.

Cultural Ecosystem Services, Social Cohesion and Community Building

The community gardening movement is offering radical new thinking, with regard to the purpose and greening of urban spaces. A new paradigm is emerging — one of a people-centred landscape; landscapes where the bland corporate style of plantings of the past are replaced with vibrant community growing spaces. These new productive spaces are being woven into urban spaces to enhance communities and provide a new aesthetic.

These community gardens allow all who attend, from people without homes, to those living in shared accommodation, to benefit from what can be considered as cultural ecosystem services. The simple act of

End of season tomatoes ripening in the productive garden at RHS Garden Harlow Carr.

gardening has been demonstrated to bring people together, tackles social exclusion and allows friendships to develop, thus meeting the social aspect of sustainability. These community gardens create a sense of place, a shared community in which all those who participate are shareholders with what is referred to as sweat equity. These garden spaces, which can be considered as patchwork farms across urban areas, also offer dispersed urban ecosystems.

Studies are showing that those who take part enjoy better mental and physical health. It is a sad reality that many less fortunate sections of society often live on heavily processed foods, as these are more affordable. A connection with productive growing improves food literacy and gives people access to fresh, nutritious, unprocessed food. Access to community kitchens within these settings allows those without kitchens or cooking equipment to produce healthy nutritious meals.

Urban green space provides cultural and environmental ecosystem services.

Case Study: Green Futures, Grimsby

Green Futures is a registered charity on the outskirts of Great Grimsby in the UK.

The team at Green Futures share a common interest and a common purpose. Each member of the team contributes to the community as they are able: some through their practical gardening knowledge, some through their ability to use and maintain equipment, while others share their joinery and construction skills, or simply their enthusiasm for being outdoors, working in a natural setting.

Volunteers join the project through word of mouth or are referred, some through green social prescribing. All benefit. During an interview, one of the participants stated, 'I would be dead if it was not for this place', indicating the vital role community horticulture plays in the lives of people. A wide range of crops is grown on-site, using organic production principles, bringing people together.

A small orchard is a community resource with festivals held to celebrate the seasons, including wassailing. Areas of woodland offer quiet spaces for reflection, greenhouses offer the opportunity to propagate plants and the larger farm areas bring people together as small teams to tackle tasks collaboratively.

Produce grown at the garden is either sold to generate funds, shared between volunteers or donated to local food banks to help alleviate food poverty and provide fresh high-quality produce to local people.

Outcomes of the service include the production of food, healthy dietary shifts, the alleviation of hunger, friendship and reducing social isolation in the community.

(Continued)

Green Futures is a registered charity on the outskirts of Great Grimsby in the UK.

Sustainability and community are at the heart of Green Futures.

Volunteers join the project and grow together, sharing a common interest and a common purpose.

Six Productive Crops to Reduce Food Miles

Thyme – growing our own herbs is an effective way to reduce food miles.

Okra 'Jing Orange', an oriental vegetable.

Courgettes work well when grown in potagers and are very productive.

Chickpeas – try growing a novel new crop every year to reduce food miles.

Peas, can be grown as pea shoots for salads.

Sweet potato can be heavy croppers.

CHAPTER 10

GARDEN MAINTENANCE

The man who moves a mountain begins by carrying away small stones.

Confucius

Garden maintenance is ultimately a series of decisions.

These decisions are ideally based on thresholds.

These thresholds are based on recording, reflecting and repeating.

Previous chapters have established that the route to sustainable garden management is based on the implementation of a million tiny decisions. This chapter considers sixty potential, sometimes tiny, changes that can be implemented to help a garden on its sustainability journey.

Sixty Steps to Sustainability

Rethink

The management of gardens can be a repetitive process, one where techniques are repeated with little thought process. This is simply the way that things are done round here. This book has advocated a deeper thought process, the rethinking and the reviewing, through fresh eyes, of every maintenance decision, in the hope that the garden can benefit, as well as the wider ecosystem.

Areas where we can rethink our maintenance options could include:

1. Considering if we should extend plantings and borders into lawned areas. This can reduce mowing, while increasing the range of ecosystem services offered by a garden. Alternatively, if the border is filled with bindweed, convert it to lawn, so you can eliminate the bindweed through mowing.
2. Reducing the extent of hard landscaping, for example the lifting of occasional paving slabs, bringing plantings into the patio and to let the patio naturally merge into plantings. These natural transition zones add to the aesthetic of the garden, and can increase biodiversity.
3. Rethinking hedge maintenance, cutting only when necessary, when fruit has been eaten by wild birds, creating an A-shape and varying the cutting zone.
4. When pruning we can apply the principles outlined in Chapter 7 and consider, for example, the needs of nesting birds, when deciding on the height that a hedge or shrub should be allowed to achieve within the garden.

Large areas of paving can be broken up with plantings to add value in aesthetics, water management and biodiversity.

5. Rather than weekly or fortnightly mowing of lawns, rethink the purpose, or potential purpose, of the grassed area. The creation of areas mown to different heights interconnected with mown paths can increase biodiversity, with longer grass favouring invertebrates, which are vital parts of the food chain.

6. When mowing, start close to the house or wall, and mow into uncut grass that is adjacent to hedges or plantings to allow small mammals to escape.

7. Grassed areas can be enriched with spring bulbs. Snowdrop, crocus or daffodil can be naturalised to provide seasonal interest and to provide important early food sources for pollinating insects.

8. Rethink container gardening. Reducing the number of containers or hanging baskets and increasing plantings in the ground. Using obelisks and other supports to add the higher-level interest lost by discontinuing hanging baskets, thus reducing inputs of growing media and water.

9. Consider replacing high water and carbon footprint bedding plants with longer lived perennials, or divisions from plants within the garden when planting up containers.

10. Apply the design practice of locating generosity within the garden. If certain plants or the presence of hanging baskets brings joy and life to an area, they can be included as exceptions to our rules, as acts of generosity to our spirits. These limited aspects can be balanced with other plantings that have positive impacts on biodiversity.

Clover Avenue, a feature at Rosemary Cottage, Hook, East Yorkshire, which is open under the National Gardens Scheme.

11. Avoid spring planting. Gardens that are sited on lighter soils, in low-rainfall regions, might wish to rethink their planting season. Autumn planting reduces the need to force plants for spring planting, which often uses fossil fuels, while also reducing the need to irrigate the plantings, thus conserving water.

12. Restraint. Are plant selections based on scientific principles rather than impulse purchases?

13. Create a cutting garden. According to the RHS website, a floral arrangement can have a carbon footprint of 7.9kg (17lb). Can we identify the working conditions of those involved in cultivating, cutting and packing those flowers? Were high inputs of synthetic fertilizers and pesticides involved in their cultivation? A final shocking statistic is that in 2022, a staggering 15,700 tonnes of flowers were airfreighted into the USA for Mother's Day. Growing a cutting garden is an effective way to combat climate change.

14. Reduce or eliminate the use of bonfires. These are polluting and unsustainable and they often injure wildlife. They can be replaced by using woody, non-compostable material to form log piles or hibernacula and on-site composting.

15. Gifting unwanted pots, garden features and tools, by donating them to horticultural charities and social enterprises; this will give the products a new lease of life, recycles and reduces waste, and helps to regenerate the organisations that are often desperate for funds.

16. Practice sustainable substitutions, such as the replacement of plastic labels with wooden ones, or the replacement of plastic string with jute or wool (pure wool rather than acrylic) when tying up plants.

17. Reduce the use of garden lighting. While there are huge emotional and aesthetic advantages in watching a garden coming to life with underlighting and other styles of light, these use energy, and so if this is an area where generosity is being applied, LED bulbs or solar battery systems are to be preferred. It should also be noted that garden lighting can also have a negative impact on wildlife. This aspect should be carefully considered, to ensure that the garden is meeting the joint needs of owner and wildlife. Compromises, such as limiting lighting to areas adjacent to buildings and the use of directional lights to reduce light spill, will ensure other garden areas are unaffected.

18. Celebrate the imperfect. Supermarkets and garden centres have influenced the way we respond to seeing insects on plants or damage on leaves. While leaf damage can be viewed as a problem to be addressed, the sustainable gardener may choose to look at the bigger picture. They may use a damaged leaf as evidence that their garden is connected to a wider ecosystem, and to view bugs as welcome guests that are part of a functioning ecosystem.

19. Paving surfaces could be softened by brushing seeds of creeping thyme, for example, into cracks, to add character and ecosystem services to areas of rustic paving. Paving areas that are prone to weeds may require repair, replacement or re-laying to negate the use of flame weeders or

Plants showing nutrient deficiencies are often the right plant in the wrong place; consider moving or replacing rather than feeding.

Gaps between paving increase drainage, preventing run-off in heavy rain. The gaps allow plants to colonize and soften the paving.

herbicides. Generous plantings can soften the effect of paving.

20. Front gardens are often overlooked or used for parking cars. Even those used for parking can be made more sustainable, ensuring that water can percolate though paving and into the soil. Planting low-growing plants where wheels do not venture can transform these spaces.

21. New garden areas, such as patios for entertaining, can apply sustainable thinking. Decking is renewable and arguably easier to install. Recycled or reclaimed paving has a lower carbon footprint. Other considerations with patios could be, what is the *minimum* size we need, maximising the area of the garden that is planted. Maintenance impacts can be minimised using mechanical brushes and watering cans, rather than caustic chemicals or pressure washers, which use both

energy and high volumes of water to keep them clean.

22. Reconsideration can be given to problem areas. However difficult the site, there are plants ideally suited for just those conditions. Researching perfect plants for problem places can be transformational.

23. Reuse and repurpose old and broken pieces of equipment. An old bucket that leaks can be used to slowly irrigate the soil adjacent to a freshly planted shrub, rather than being disposed of. Old wheelbarrows can be planted or filled with logs to create habitats.

Reduce and Reuse

We can reduce the carbon and water footprint of our garden by carefully considering every input to the

An old mini has become a planter, in this Chelsea Flower Show Garden. Less extreme use of old items as planters is perhaps more appropriate!

garden, from replacing bagged growing media with home-made, or repairing and sharpening ageing garden tools. Once the concept of reduce, reuse and recycle becomes second nature, the process of gardening with ingenuity becomes more rewarding than simply buying new equipment.

1. Reducing inputs into the garden is one of the core principles of sustainable gardening. Therefore, creating a small nursery area, where plants can be propagated and grown, can reduce the water, carbon and plastic footprints of the garden.

2. Hanging baskets included as a location of generosity in the design of the garden require regular feeding and watering. The quantities of liquid feed and water can be reduced by placing a bucket under the basket to capture any liquid that drains through, which can be used on the next container or saved for the following day.

3. To make major reductions in inputs, the requirements of different garden areas should be assessed. This process can then inform value judgements to be made. It may be that the rose garden requires considerable inputs in time, chemicals to fight blackspot or pesticide to control greenfly. Measuring these inputs allows us to prioritise areas for review. It allows for the consideration of more sustainable interventions. It also allows the question: do we really want this area of garden, if it needs such a high level of intervention? A scoring system could be developed to measure inputs against outputs, to determine the point where a feature should be removed.

4. The incidence of pest and diseases can be reduced through the practice of good garden-based hygiene. This includes the quarantine of new plants, vigilance and the sterilisation of all garden tools used, for example in pruning and the training of plants. Sustainable sterilising materials can include the use of alcohol-based hand gels or the spraying of rubbing alcohol or vinegar, which should then be wiped off with a cloth.

5. Water usage can be reduced through the selection of appropriate plant species, and through the use of deep mulches. Mulches insulate the ground from excessive heat in the summer and excessive cold in the winter, while sealing moisture into the garden to create habitats for numerous invertebrate species, and decomposes to form humic substances that enhance soil structure.

6. The density of plantings can also impact on management inputs. Plants that are planted loosely allow the sun to reach the soil but have lower water and nutritional demands on the soil. The looser plantings often allow the growth of spontaneous plants. Tighter, higher density plantings result in reduced evaporation from the soil, and increased demand from plant roots for water and nutrients. The layering of plants also impacts on this balance. The correct planting densities can be reached through an in-depth knowledge of the site and the characteristics of the plants being cultivated. A useful rule of thumb

with the planting of perennials is to plant at seven or nine plants per square metre.

7. Buy small. Garden centres and nurseries are often filled with large plants, grown in large pots, with equally large plastic, carbon and water footprints. Smaller plants will often grow away better if appropriate to the site conditions and outperform those planted in larger containers. A perennial grown in a 7cm (3in) liner or square pot, is both cheaper and more sustainable than one in a 3 or 5ltr container.

8. Water usage can be reduced. Careful plant selection, soil management and other techniques, discussed in Chapter 11, can be applied. Water butts or the use of universal bulk containers (UBCs), which can store 1,000ltr (220gal) of water should be considered. Adding these to the downpipes from garden buildings can result in a network of water storage containers in the garden. UBCs (positioned out of sight) add the advantage of storing large volumes of water, with the fact that they are repurposed and are not, therefore, adding to the volumes of plastic on the planet.

9. Bird tables and feeders can be vital food sources for wild birds; however, they can also result in the spreading of disease, especially after sick birds have visited. This risk can be reduced by regular (monthly) cleaning down with a disinfectant solution.

10. Collecting and saving home-grown seeds reduces inputs and saves money. Seeds can easily be stored in old coffee jars, with a sachet of water-retaining gel, which can be reused from the packaging of shoes or electrical goods.

11. Repurpose items to create sculptural interest in the garden.

Regenerate

The following concepts can be used as part of the role of the garden in regeneration, and the provision of plantings and features to enhance biodiversity.

1. Roof areas can have wooden seed trays fitted, which when filled with sedum or similar species, increases habitats and provides pollen and nectar.

2. Replace small areas of gravel with plantings that provide distinct ecosystem services, such as

teasels for goldfinches or ornamental thistles for their fluffy seed heads.

3. Practise mindfulness to regenerate the mind and enhance mental health, 'garden less, enjoy more is the new mantra'.

4. Minimal interventions allow plantings to develop to provide cover and habitat that is in itself regenerative to a number of different species.

5. Small areas of moist or wet soil can be created. These areas are perfect for house martins and swallows to forage for nest building, and for amphibians to use as cool damp places, which are even better if under leaf cover.

6. Add a range of nesting boxes for birds and bats, or small bug hotels to allow insects to overwinter in the garden.

7. Bumble bees often nest in hollows adjacent to clumps of long grass. Creating such habitats can

Bird feeding stations can be integrated into plantings.

In this garden, old cutlery has been repurposed to create mock *Agapanthus* and add a sense of fun to the plantings.

encourage bumblebee colonies in the garden, helping with the regeneration of this species.

8. Regenerate soil, but with deep mulching to avoid the carbon release from digging.
9. Create areas where you can lose yourself either in simple gardening tasks or where you can sit and watch bees, butterflies and birds.
10. Do not be too hasty to rake up leaves; if they will not smother surrounding plants, then leave them to decompose slowly and incorporate into the soil. The decomposing leaf litter offers a valuable habitat for invertebrates and a food source for microorganisms.
11. Bird baths provide both bathing and drinking water for wild birds. Saucers with gravel allow hydration stations for bees, butterflies and moths to be created.
12. Plant crevices of walls with *Aubretia* or other similar plantings to add ecosystem services.
13. Use wire hoops within plantings to encourage spiders to form webs within the garden.
14. Learn to identify beneficial insects, to ensure that these are not removed in error.
15. Recycle prunings creatively. They can be used to great effect to add height to containers, as woven skirts and as plant supports.

Record, Reflect Repeat

1. Keep a diary to record new spontaneous plant species that have arrived in the garden, or sightings of wildlife.

One of the roof areas at Great Dixter, planted up to provide ecosystem services.

If fallen leaves are not damaging low-growing plants, leave them on borders to decompose and be incorporated into the soil.

Gardeners at RHS Garden Hyde Hall use prunings from *Cornus* (dog wood) to provide height, colour and a sculptural element to planters.

2. Set measurable goals for the garden: to attract goldfinches, to be adopted by hedgehogs or to grow your own herbs to reduce food miles.
3. Carry out a baseline survey of the plant species in the garden, along with the wildlife that visits the garden, to set a benchmark.
4. Blog or share your sustainability adventure with the hashtag (#thenewwaytogarden).
5. Follow #thenewwaytogarden to connect with like-minded people who are on the same sustainability journey.
6. To what extent have you conformed to the principles outlined in this book? Record the easy wins, reflect on the tougher, failed challenges, rethink approaches and research new perspectives. Apply forgiveness. Sustainability is a never-ending journey.
7. Record challenges and achievable goals for the next year, to ensure that the journey continues and that the garden becomes a greater force for change.
8. Carry out an annual review of the Garden Health Plan. Were all issues recorded? Were all interventions recorded?
9. Record changes within the garden. Does the soil drain more easily? Does this area of garden look fuller and have a better aesthetic?
10. Record the areas where generosity has been applied and where sustainable rules have been relaxed. Review these areas. Have you planned in enough generosity? Have you planned in too much?

CHAPTER 11

WATER IN THE GARDEN

We forget that the water cycle and the life cycle are one.

Jacques-Yves Cousteau

Sources of Water

The management of water within gardens is becoming increasingly important as a changing climate is resulting in gardens having to be able to withstand both periods of prolonged drought, with short, high rainfall events increasing. This changing weather pattern is not only affecting gardens but the supply of water from reservoirs and other sources. Water management is, therefore, climbing up the priority list for all those who manage gardens and green spaces. Current sources of water in the UK include rainfall, captured rainfall, boreholes, extraction from rivers or the use of mains water. Each of these sources of water poses its own problems.

- Rainfall is no longer reliable as a source of water for some plantings within gardens, especially those on lighter soils or on the drier east coast regions.
- Rainwater capture deprives the local environment of water, as the water is diverted from percolating through the soil into storage containers. Rainwater

capture is proving at times to be unable to meet the needs of gardens during extended periods of drought. These negative impacts of water capture on-site can be balanced by the environmental benefit that filling of storage containers plays during major rainfall events. The volume of water captured is the volume of water that is now held back and not causing issues with flooding, either within the garden or in other lower lying gardens.

- Boreholes, where licensed, allow for the extraction of water from underground sources. A borehole is sunk, usually 50—80m (164—262ft) into the ground. A small pump is placed at the bottom of the shaft, and water is pumped to a storage tank ready for use. This water is often considered to be sustainable, as it comes from within the garden; it is also claimed to have a lower carbon footprint, as there is less energy input in filtering and pumping. As this water is being extracted from deep into the ground, it is also claimed to protect local wetlands and their associated ecosystems. It should be noted that this extraction of water in coastal areas can result in the drawing in of saline water, which impacts negatively on plant growth. Water scientists increasingly view the water extracted using techniques such as this as being fossil water. This is considered to be non-renewable water. Its use denies future generations the opportunity to make use of this resource, which makes this a problematic source of water from a sustainability perspective.

- The extraction of water from rivers, where licensed, removes water from the local environment. This can impact on the local ecology or on the ecology of habitats downstream. While this impact is taken into account when granting extraction licences, this issue highlights the potential environmental impacts of using river water for irrigation. It has been estimated that an average person uses 140ltr (31gal) of water a day. A lawn sprinkler, in comparison, can use 1,000ltr (220gal) of water an hour. This means that one hour of irrigating a lawn with a sprinkler is equivalent to a week's use of water for an average person.

In decorative areas water butts can be matched to the greenhouse structure to make a pleasing design.

Universal bulk containers can be used to store large volumes of water. While plastic, they are repurposed, and so do not increase the amount of plastic on the planet. They are suitable for working, rather than decorative areas.

The extraction of water from rivers can impact on the local ecology, or on the ecology of habitats downstream; it is, therefore, regarded as an unsustainable practice.

Reducing the Water Footprint

Every source of water has an ecological footprint. Indeed, the UK Wildlife Trusts suggest that reducing water usage to keep more water in our ecosystems will keep wetlands topped up, which would benefit wildlife such as otters, water voles, herons and fish, amongst countless other species. Garden managers are now increasingly looking at methods that can be used to reduce the water footprint of gardens. Some measures, such as mulching or the procurement of smaller bare-root plants, have already been considered. Other mitigations to reduce the use of water in gardens include:

- Decide where to locate generosity: is there a particular garden area that is of significance, which should continue to receive this input, concentrating water-reduction strategies on other areas of the garden.
- Measure and record the water input into each bed or garden area. This can be achieved by using a simple digital flow meter that is added to the tap.
- Reduce the water footprint of the garden by reducing areas devoted to short-term, seasonal plantings, which require water to aid establishment.
- Line clay or other porous pots with plastic to reduce evaporation of water from the surface of the pot. Gardeners in cooler climates may wish to consider lining pots with bubble plastic, which provides the roots of the plants with frost protection over the winter.
- If new plantings are being created on lighter soils, using irrigation pipes that weep water into the rootzone may be appropriate.
- Care should be taken when irrigating to ensure minimal applications of water, to cut down, not only on the volume of water used, but also on the potential of fertilizer leaching out of the growing medium.
- Floating mulches can be used to lower the water demand in recently planted areas. Floating mulches can be purchased for reuse from field-scale vegetable production to reduce the environmental impact of manufacture.
- If the site is windy, then the planting of a shelterbelt or windbreak can filter wind, and so reduce the drying effect

- If extending the seasonal interest in a border, such as for late summer interest, keep these plants together in one location to reduce the need to irrigate the whole border.
- If renovating and replanting a border, water can be saved by carrying out this process over three or five years instead of one year. Each section that requires irrigation to establish will thus be reduced, which may mean that the water captured on-site may be sufficient.
- Allow lawns to turn yellow, which can be considered to be heat-induced dormancy, a survival characteristic of grass. It will green up quickly when the rains return.
- Finally, and perhaps most significantly, match the plant specification to the site characteristics. If the site is on lighter, sandy soils and in the east of the country, then consider drought-tolerant plants. While these require a longer establishment period while they develop their extensive root systems, once established they have a minimal need for water.

The management of water in the garden also includes developing strategies to cope with areas of water-logging. Large-scale drainage systems are often problematic within garden settings as there is nowhere for the captured water to escape. The installation of drainage schemes causes soil disturbance and so releases carbon, and the pipes involved are often plastic. A more sustainable option is to see the potential of the site as an area where plants that require

Irrigation systems that supply water to the rootzone can both reduce water usage and help with plant establishment.

Floating mulches can lower water demand in newly planted areas.

Matching the planting to the soil conditions and annual rainfall will dramatically reduce water usage.

waterlogged soils can be grown, possibly creating a small wetland habitat.

Rain Gardens

At their simplest, rain gardens are shallow, hollow areas. They can be planted with species that are able to withstand temporary flooding, such as *Miscanthus*, *Iris*, *Rudbeckia* and *Euphorbia* sp.. These gardens are best situated at least 3m (10ft) from a building to prevent potential damage to foundations and be able to slowly dissipate water into the soil over periods of time. Some rain gardens are situated away from buildings, with dry riverbeds carrying storm water into the shallow, hollow areas, which are called swales. Rain gardens should not be installed near to a septic tank or other similar systems, and slopes are best avoided.

The concept of a rain garden can be applied to planters that are placed close to buildings:

- These structures are often made of timber.
- They have a solid base with a layer of gravel to provide drainage.
- They are filled to within 5—7cm (2—3in) of the top with a soil-based growing medium.
- The down pipe is adapted to run into the upper surface of the container.
- An additional section of downpipe is added at the surface of the container, which connects to the original downpipe to carry excess water away.
- The container is filled with shrubs or perennials.

These containers, which are gaining popularity in urban areas, allow rainfall to be diverted from the drainage system, to irrigate and fill the container with water. Only in very high rainfall, when the container is at capacity, does the water get diverted into the urban drainage system/sewer.

Rain Garden Rules

The RHS recommends testing the soil to make sure it is appropriate for a rain garden. Simply dig a hole, fill it with water and time how long it takes to empty.

If the water level drops 12—50mm per hour, then the site (if it meets other location criteria) is considered to be ideal for a rain garden.

Rain Garden Size

Best practice suggests that rain gardens should occupy 20 per cent of the total roof area of the house or shed. A shed with 20 square metres of roof area would, therefore, require a 4 square metre rain garden.

Watering cans are more efficient than hosepipes, if irrigation is required (Great Dixter Garden).

Chains incorporated in downpipes can lead water into rain gardens.

CHAPTER 12

HABITAT CREATION

The one process now going on that will take millions of years to correct is the loss of genetic and species diversity by the destruction of natural habitats. This is the folly our descendants are least likely to forgive us.

E. O. Wilson

The Royal Society reports that Britain is home to more than 70,000 known species of animals, plants, fungi and microorganisms. This number fell by 13 per cent between the 1970s and 2019. It may seem ambitious to think that garden owners and managers can impact on these figures and trends. However, the RHS reports that 88 per cent of households in the UK have access to a private or shared garden, and that the total area of gardens in the UK is 700,000ha. If just 10 per cent of these gardens were to create habitats, that would be the same as a chain of micro-nature reserves covering 70,000ha.

While it is second nature to provide bird feeding stations or install bug hotels and hedgehog houses, the creation of habitat can seem daunting. Good questions might be:

- What habitat?
- For which species?
- To what end?

Small bug hotels made with material foraged from within the garden can provide an excellent habitat for overwintering insects. They are best emptied and refreshed with new material annually to reduce the incidence of parasitic mites.

The UK Biodiversity Action Plan (BAP) identifies priority habitats and priority species of plants, animals and fungi. When considering the creation of habitats in gardens, reference to BAPs can inform decisions and so benefit priority species. When large garden developments are undertaken, for example the development of the RHS Garden Bridgewater, BAPs are used to inform design decisions. The garden carried out an initial survey to identify the biodiversity of the site to establish a baseline. The management team then identified priority habitats from the UK BAP, to inform design decisions prior to the garden build commencing. The key priority habitats in the UK, which could be contained within gardens include:

- Rivers and streams.
- Standing open water.
- Hedgerows.
- Traditional orchards.
- Woodland.
- Meadows.
- Heathland.

Woodland is a UK BAP priority habitat.

Key priority species, which could benefit from garden habitat, include:

- West European hedgehog.
- Dormouse.
- Bats (various species).
- Slow-worm.
- Natterjack toad.
- Common toad.
- Red star thistle.
- Cornflower.
- Brown-banded carder bee.
- Large garden bumblebee.
- Short-haired bumblebee.

Every Garden, Everywhere

Habitat can be created within larger public gardens or can be scaled down to fit in to even the smallest of courtyard gardens. While standing water in a 150ha garden or designed landscape is of great ecological significance, a small washing-up bowl, sunk in a tiny courtyard can become an urban wildlife oasis.

Eight Great Habitats to Create

Hedgerows
Species-rich hedgerows are defined by the UK Habitat Action Plan as ones that contain five or more native woody species in a 30m (98ft) length. Hedges with fewer species than this, but which are augmented by having herbaceous perennials growing at the base of the hedge, are also considered species rich.

It is worth noting that species that make up the hedge should all offer considerable ecosystem services; therefore yew, privet and beech hedging are excluded.

The Royal Society for the Protection of Birds (RSPB) reports that hedges support up to 80 per cent of our woodland birds, 50 per cent of our mammals and 30 per cent of butterflies. Hedges do not have to be high, with 2m (6½ft) high hedging providing nesting sites for species such as yellowhammers and linnets. The impact of hedges as habitat is greatly increased when they have wide bases. Herbaceous perennials extend the habitat of the hedge, providing cover for mammals such as wood mice and hedgehogs, and providing food sources for insect larvae that form part of the food chain/web.

Butterfly City

Kingston upon Hull has set out to be the first Butterfly City in the UK.

Community groups and residents have planted over 3,000 alder buckthorn in the city, to encourage brimstone butterflies to the city.

Butterfly City logo.

Hedgerow species to support biodiversity

Alder Buckthorn (*Frangula alnus*) An ideal hedging plant, especially for damper sites. This species is the food source for the larvae of the brimstone butterfly, as well as a nectar source for bees.

Common Hawthorn (*Crataegus monogyna*) Hawthorn can support a wide range of wildlife: dormice eat the flowers, bees and other pollinating insects benefit from pollen and nectar from flowers in May, while the leaves feed a wide range of bugs and caterpillars. The haws (berries) are eaten by wild birds. The thorny stems provide nesting shelter for many species of bird.

Dog Rose (*Rosa canina*) The dog rose is a climber that has large pink to white flowers in the spring and red, oval, berry-like fruit in the autumn. The flowers provide pollen and nectar for pollinating species, while the fruits are quickly ripped open to reveal the seeds, which are food sources for blackbirds and other species of wild bird.

Field Maple (*Acer campestre*) The field maple has a dense canopy made up of small leaves. It often supports (like many species of *Acer*) large populations of aphids, which are in turn predated on by ladybirds, lacewings and hoverflies. Insectivorous birds also predate on the aphids, using them as an important food source when rearing chicks. The flowers provide nectar and pollen, and the fruit/seeds produced are food sources for small mammals.

Holly (*Ilex aquifolium*) The simple leaves with spines on holly provide cover and ideal nesting opportunities for birds. The leaf litter at the base of holly is often used by small mammals and hedgehogs for hibernation. The flowers provide pollen and nectar for pollinating species, the leaves support holly leaf miner and are eaten by the caterpillars of the holly blue butterfly and several species of moth. The berries are important food sources for a wide range of wildlife, from birds to woodmice and dormice, both priority species in the UK BAP.

Ivy (*Hedera helix*) While many gardeners battle with ivy, it is a very important species when creating a habitat. The UK Wildlife Trusts suggest that it may support up to fifty wildlife species. Ivy flowers late in the year, during autumn and winter, making it an important food source for many different pollinators. The leaves are an important food source for numerous butterfly and moth caterpillars. The berries have a high fat content and so are an important high-calorie food source for wild birds.

Honeysuckle (*Lonicera periclymenum*) While this might not be the first species that comes to mind when planning a hedge planting, it flowers over a long period and is of significant value to wildlife. Some butterfly species (such as the rare white admiral) rely solely on honeysuckle, while other visitors include bumblebees of many species. It is an important habitat for dormice, who use the bark for nesting, and whose young eat the sweet nectar-rich flowers. A wide range of birds and moths also rely on honeysuckle.

Traveller's Joy/Old Man's Beard (*Clematis vitalba*) The seed heads, from which the name old man's beard is derived, are prized as food sources by goldfinches, the flowers are popular food sources with bees and hoverflies, and the leaves support a large range of butterfly and moth caterpillars.

Wayfaring Tree (*Viburnum lantana*) This viburnum produces a large number of white flowers, which are important food sources for both bees and butterflies. The leaves are important food sources for several moth species and the berries (which start red, and turn black) are an important food source for wild birds.

Still Freshwater

Areas of still freshwater used to be common features of the UK landscape. Dew ponds, which were often situated on higher ground, were used for supplying water to livestock, with natural ponds situated in hollows and dips. These ponds provide drinking water for wild birds and provide a habitat for dragonflies and a wide range of aquatic invertebrates. They are breeding grounds for frogs, newts and toads. Some studies suggest that dew ponds alone can support approximately 70 per cent of all freshwater species found in lowland landscapes. Ecologists argue that the benefit of these ponds increases significantly when there is a network of them in an area, making it easy for species to move between them. A network of local ponds (e.g. in gardens) is also seen as adding resilience to local climate change. Sadly, we have lost 70 per cent of ponds from the UK landscape in the last 100 years, which explains why the creation of still freshwater is a priority.

Creating a Wildlife Pond

- In nature, ponds would form in shallow dips and lower points in the landscape; therefore, ponds

We have lost 70 per cent of ponds from the UK landscape in the last 100 years.

that are sited in hollows or dips in the garden have a natural 'always been there' look to them.

- Ponds can be of almost any size and shape, ideally following the contour of the land.
- To provide an ideal habitat for wildlife, ponds should be excavated to 20—60cm (8—24in). Thought should be given as to how the soil that is excavated can be used within the garden, to avoid the transportation of soil out of the garden.
- While preformed plastic or fibreglass ponds are widely available, along with butyl rubber liners, these materials cannot be recycled easily and so should be considered a last resort (the positive environmental benefits of the pond will outweigh the environmental footprint of the liner). Sustainable liners include puddled clay or sodium bentonite, which is a clay-based product that creates an effective liner for ponds and lakes.
- Wildlife using the pond will require a shallow sloping side, which allows safe access and egress to the water. If this is problematic because of site limitations, then a wooden scaffolding board can be weighted and lowered into the pond to enable egress.
- The use of pebbles near to the water surface creates a perfect environment for bees and other insects to access the water. If these areas of dry pebble, with water between, are situated close to seating areas, then one can enjoy the sight of bees lining up to access the water.

- The water level in ponds can vary according to rainfall and sun. Ponds that look natural have turf or plantings laid to conceal the liner.
- Wildlife ponds are part of the overall garden ecosystem and should connect to other wildlife habitats. A pond surrounded by paving on all sides or close-mown grass, will not connect into the garden ecosystem as deeply as one that has shrubs for cover and perching close to it, or that connects with a wildflower meadow.
- Newly constructed ponds can be left for plants and wildlife to colonise this new ecological feature or can be planted up. The RHS recommend four plant types:
  - Underwater plants that both create cover for wildlife and provide oxygen.
  - Plants that emerge through the water for aquatic larvae to crawl up, to enable them to enter the adult stage of their life cycle.
  - Plants with leaves that float on the surface of the water to provide cover and places for wildlife to rest.
  - Pollinator-friendly marginal plantings that include both sources of pollen and also food sources for caterpillars.

A plank in a pond allows animals, like hedgehogs, that have fallen into the pond to escape.

A shallow, sloping beach is advised to allow animals to drink from the pond edge and exit the water.

Streams

The Freshwater Habitats Trust reports that 87 per cent of headwater streams are biologically degraded east of a line from the Humber to the Dorset coast. Streams are defined as bodies of water less than 8.25m (27ft) in width, often do not follow field boundaries (as ditches would), running instead along contours or down valleys. They provide an important habitat for species that require running water.

Streams can be added within gardens to connect bodies of water or as part of the installation of rain gardens, to manage water retention. They do not have to have water in them at all times, being landscaped to resemble dry riverbeds when not in use holding or transporting water.

Wildflower Meadow

Wildflower meadows, filled with a range of annual or perennial plants that provide nectar for pollinating insects, egg-laying habits and food sources for caterpillars, are important in the creation of garden ecosystems. These habitats also provide spaces that are colonised by spiders, ladybirds and lacewings, which provide pest-control services within the garden. These important habitats also provide a source of both food and nesting material for wild birds, and cover for small mammals.

They become more significant habitats when they connect areas such as hedgerows with water sources, such as streams and ponds.

Perennial meadows are discussed in more detail in Chapter 6.

Heathland

This lowland habitat occurs on acidic, dry or impoverished soils, which can be sandy, or peat-based. Heathland can often be identified by the vegetation associated with it, which includes heather and gorse, as well as the edible bilberry. Heathland has become a rare and threatened environment: 84 per cent of heathland has been lost since 1800. It is an important habitat, as it is home to sand lizards, smooth snakes, nightjars and the Dartford warbler.

Gardens with heathland soils often attempt significant soil amelioration to create ecologically inappropriate plantings, for example the creation of rose gardens, which consume large volumes of water that is unsustainable. The sustainable mantra is to play the cards one is dealt and see the opportunities this hand allows. If one is given heathland, then this should be celebrated, if the space allows, by creating a specialist garden area filled with heathland plants, such as heathers, lings, dog violets, harebells and meadowsweet.

Woodland Edge

Many gardens can be considered to be woodland edge. These habitats are generally made up of three layers of plantings. If there is space available in the garden then a tree layer can be planted; however, smaller gardens will find a hedgerow to be equally effective. The next layer, from a height perspective, is the shrub layer, with an herbaceous layer completing the planting. A ground-cover layer, planted with spring bulbs or other ground-cover plants, will create additional habitats and provide additional food sources for wildlife.

A garden with these elements will have a wide range of habitats. With careful selection of plants that provide ecosystem services, this specialist garden area can become an even richer and more significant habitat.

The Wildlife Trusts in the UK report that oak trees support 284 different insect species. Smaller trees also provide nesting and perching sites, and provide food sources, including caterpillars eating their leaves, nectar and fruit. Hawthorn, apples, holly and rowan are excellent smaller trees. Climbing plants, such as bramble and honeysuckle, add additional sources of food. Shrubs such as berberis and dog woods and the guelder rose enhance the offer of the area to wildlife. The

Rivers can be added to gardens, to direct water to rain gardens, or connect ponds.

Allium 'Forelock' attracting a bee in a wildflower meadow.

herbaceous layer can be planted with biennials, such as foxgloves. Nettles provide habitat for around forty species of insect, which in turn attract wild birds. Other suitable plants can include the candytuft or specific plant species to attract specific desirable species of wildlife.

The habitat potential of woodland-edge gardens can be enhanced with log piles, hibernacula, which can support up to 400 species of saproxylic invertebrates (those that live on dead wood), including the stag beetle. Nesting boxes, bat boxes and roughly cut bundles of hollow stems for overwintering insects also create valuable habitat.

The potential of woodland edge gardens can be increased with minimal interventions. Fallen leaves provide a perfect environment for many invertebrates. Hollow stems, chopped and dropped, provide habitat for solitary bees. Log piles favour beetles, toads and small mammals. Decomposing leaf litter will often be colonised by brandling worms, which in turn are a food source for hedgehogs, a priority species in the UK Biodiversity Action Plan.

Woodland-edge gardens adjacent to streams and ponds can be even richer and more diverse habitats.

Managed Woodland

Small gardens can have tiny, managed woodlands. Coppicing (where the tree is cut to the ground and the wood is harvested) is an effective management technique for these areas. Trees that are suitable for coppice include hazel, eucalyptus, hornbeam and willow. Coppiced woodland lends itself to understorey plantings with, for example, primrose.

A small woodland of five trees could be coppiced with one tree cut back to the ground each year, resulting in a harvest of stems that can be used in productive and other garden settings. This use of home-grown plant supports offers considerable benefit compared with the harvest and transport of bamboo canes, which come with a considerable environmental and carbon footprint.

A key advantage of small, coppiced garden areas is that the trees grown in this way have reduced canopies (compared to trees that are not coppiced). The reduced canopy allows greater light to reach the ground, resulting in a wider range of sub-shrubs or herbaceous plant growth, which in turn offers benefit to insects, butterflies, birds, bats and mammals.

Traditional Orchard

Traditional orchards are significantly different from the commercial monocultures involved in fruit production from an ecological perspective. They are made up of small trees, which grow in a matrix of grasses, wildflowers and small shrubs. They are often surrounded by hedges or windbreaks, and at their best have small ponds. The trees in orchards are planted at low densities, allowing more light to pass through the canopy and reach the ground. This allows a richer diversity of wildflowers to grow within a matrix of grasses amongst the trees. It also favours species that benefit from being able to warm themselves in sunshine, such as some species of bee and butterflies.

Fruit trees make a particularly rich habitat as the blossom offers ecosystem services, boosts wellness and produces pollen and nectar. The trees themselves are productive and offer a local food source for both people and wildlife. The greatest significance of traditional orchards, however, is that the trees age very quickly, resulting in dead wood, hollow branches and trunks, and holes made by the rotting of wood, rough bark, dead wood and areas where sap has run down the trunk. While, from a traditional plant health perspective, dead wood and holes are best avoided, they do make excellent habitats. This perhaps sums up the dilemma between traditional garden thinking that was focused on perfection and the new thinking that is focused on habitat and biodiversity, as these tree defects support species of bat, lesser spotted woodpecker and smaller owls.

Saproxylic Beetles

These beetles lay their eggs under the bark or within dead wood. Beetle authority Dr Ross Piper explains on his blog-based website that 650 beetle species from fifty-three families are associated with dead wood. Some of these beetles feed directly on the dead wood, others feed on the fungi breaking down the dead wood or growing in the root cavities of standing trees. Some are hunters and feed on the species that are feeding on the dead wood and fungi. Further details of Dr Piper's website, including identification guides to beetles, are included in the 'Further Resources' at the end of this book.

Brown Hedges

Brown hedges are simple to install and provide a habitat for a range of invertebrates, amphibians and small mammals. Low, brown hedges can edge borders; taller ones can divide off spaces.

Poles can be pushed into the ground to create a framework for a brown hedge (RHS Garden Wisley).

Prunings are then woven into the gap between the poles to create the hedge (RHS Garden Wisley).

The completed brown hedge, ready to provide a range of ecosystem services (RHS Garden Wisley).

SUSTAINABILITY ASSESSMENT TOOL

This book has been written to provide guidance to garden owners and garden managers to enable them as they progress on their sustainability journey. This appendix proposes a Sustainability Assessment Tool. The concept behind this tool is to allow a gardener to pause, put the kettle on and then take stock of where they are on their individual sustainability journey. A number of criteria are suggested, but these are not set in stone and can be changed to suit the style of the garden and the interest of the gardener. The key principle is to carry out a fact-based audit to measure the distance travelled, and to set year on year improvement targets. While it is accepted that gardeners could meet together and audit each other, the intent behind the SAT is simply to allow for reflection and celebration of achievement.

Initial assessment:

Sustainability Assessment Tool

Assessment of Quality		
To what extent has the sustainability journey impacted on the quality of the garden?		
Criteria	Measure	Score x 10
Social — have key suppliers been audited to ensure that all people in the supply chain are treated equally?	Are UK staff paid the living wage? Do key suppliers refer to the Modern Slavery Act on their website? How well is the welfare of people working down the supply chain ensured?	

Energy	Is the energy used within the garden (e.g. electricity) from renewable sources? What proportion of energy used in the garden comes from fossil fuels? Has the carbon footprint of the garden been calculated or approximated?	
Water usage	What volume of water was used in the garden the previous year? What volume of water has been used this year? What is the percentage reduction in water usage?	
Tool replacement	Is sustainability taken into account when procuring new tools? Has full life-cycle assessment or a similar model been used to ensure end of life recycling?	
Plant procurement	To what extent is plant procurement based on: Site characteristics? Peat and plastic-free production? Local production? From local nurseries that pay the staff the living wage?	
Short-term plantings	How many short-term plants were procured last year? How many short-term plants were procured this year? What is the year-on-year reduction?	
Fertilizer usage	How many kg/lb of fertilizer were used last year? How many kg/lb of fertilizer were used this year? What is the year-on-year reduction?	
Pesticide usage	Were IPM and Garden Health Plan records kept up to date over the year? Were any insecticides, fungicides or herbicides used during the year?	
Areas of longer grass	Have mowing regimes been amended to benefit wildflowers? Results of quadrat survey — no. of wildflowers per square metre over average lawn areas? Has mowing been reduced during the year? Is grass cut to a variety of heights?	
Habitat creation	How many different habitats are present in the garden? Has this number changed in the last year? Have wildlife sightings increased or decreased over the year?	

Total score for year:

BIBLIOGRAPHY

Chapter 1 Understanding Sustainability

Capdevila-Cortada, M., *'Electrifying the Haber—Bosch'* (nature.com 2019) (accessed December 2022)

Carson, R., *Silent Spring* (Penguin Modern Classics, 2000)

Ethical Trading Initiative (ethicaltrade.org) (accessed December 2022)

Marshalls, *'Respecting People'* (marshalls.co.uk) (accessed December 2022)

McMillan, P., Roach M., *'Natural Community Gardening'* (awaytogarden.com 2021) (accessed December 2022)

Mind, *'Over 7 million have taken up gardening since the pandemic: new research shows spending more time in nature has boosted nation's well-being'* (mind.org.uk, 2022) (accessed December 2022)

Mollison, B., Holmgren, D., *Permaculture One* (Corgi, 1978)

Muir, J., *My First Summer in the Sierra* (Houghton Mifflin, 1911)

Newton, I., Personal comms (Robert Hooke), 1675

NHS, *'Green Social Prescribing'* (England.nhs.uk) (accessed December 2022)

Royal Horticultural Society, *'A new report, released in September 2021, outlines how the ornamental horticulture and landscaping industry is set to contribute nearly £42 billion to the UK and support more than 760,000 jobs by 2030'* (rhs.org.uk) (accessed December 2022)

Rumsfled, D., *Pentagon Briefing* (CNN transcripts, 2002 transcripts.cnn.com) (accessed December 2022)

World Commission on Environment and Development, *Our Common Future* (United Nations, 1987)

Chapter 2 It All Starts With Good Design Decisions

Masaaki, I., *Kaizen: The Key to Japan's Competitive Success* (McGraw-Hill, 1986)

Parliamentary Office of Science and Technology, *'Ecosystem Service Valuation'* (POSTNOTE 378, 2011)

Royal Horticultural Society, *'Gardening in a Changing Climate'* (rhs.org.uk) (accessed December 2022)

Royal Horticultural Society, *'Working with nature, from increasing biodiversity to managing water, sustainability and caring for the landscape are key to what we do at RHS Garden Bridgewater'* (rhs.org.uk) (accessed December 2022)

Chapter 3 Soil: The Unseen Ecosystem

Lal, R., 'The Solution Under Our Feet: How Regenerative Organic Agriculture Can Save the Planet' (ecowatch.com, 2015) (accessed December 2022)

Merrifield, K., 'The Secret Life of Soil' (oeregonstate.edu, 2010) (accessed December 2022)

Rothamsted Research, 'Fertilizers Reduce Plant-Beneficial Bacteria Found Around Roots' (rothamsted.ac.uk, 2021) (accessed December 2022)

Sustainable Soils Alliance, Facts and Figures (sustainablesoils.org) (accessed December 2022)

UK Government, 'How to Produce a Soil-Management Plan' (gov.co.uk) (accessed December 2022)

Chapter 4 Plants and Planting

Attenborough, D., Planet Earth II (BBC, 2016)

Cameron, R., The Modern Garden Conference — Planting for a Changing Climate (Plant Network, 2021)

Irish Peat Conservation Council, 'Peatlands as Climate Sinks' (ipcc.ie) (accessed December 2022)

Korn, P., 'Enter Sandman: The High Diversity Plantings of Peter Korn', (thenewperennialist.com 2022) (accessed December 2022)

Korn, P, 'Giving Plants What They Want', 2013

UK Government, 'Modern Slavery Act 2015' (Legislation.gov.uk) (accessed December 2022)

Watkins, H, 'Gardeners Question Time' (BBC Radio 4, 2022)

The Wildlife Trusts, 'Natural Solutions to the Climate Crisis — Peatlands' (wildlifetrusts.org) (accessed December 2022)

Chapter 5 Garden Health

BBC, 'Highest Temperature on Earth as Death Valley, US hits 54.4C' (bbc.co.uk, 2020) (accessed December 2022)

Cambridge University Botanic Garden, 'White Willow (Salix alba)' (botanic.cam.ac.uk) (accessed December 2022)

De Morgan, A., A Budget of Paradoxes (Longmans, Green and Co., 1872)

DEFRA, 'UK Plant Health Risk Register' (planthealthportal.defra.gov.uk) (accessed December 2022)

Chapter 6 Sustainable Lawn Management

Aspen, aspenfuel.co.uk (accessed December 2022)

Bacon, F., 'Essays' 1625

Christensen A., Westerholm R., Almén J., 'Measurement of Regulated and Unregulated Exhaust Emissions from a Lawn Mower with and without an Oxidizing Catalyst: A Comparison of Two Different Fuels', Environ. Sci. Technol. (American Chemical Society) 2001

Hitchler, L., 'Grass Lawns are an Ecological Catastrophe' (ONE Only Natural Energy 2018, onlynaturalenergy.com) (accessed December 2022)

Morgan S., Stoddart K., The Climate Change Garden (Green Rocket, 2019)

Natural History Museum, 'Natural History Museum reveals the world has crashed through the "safe limit for humanity" for biodiversity loss' (nhm.ac.uk 2021) (accessed December 2022)

Plantlife, 'What is Every Flower Counts?' (nomowmay.plantlife.org.uk) (accessed December 2022)

Wright, F. L., Lecture to students at Guggenheim Museum, Guggenheim.org (accessed December 2022)

Chapter 7 Principles of Pruning

Felco, (felco.com) (accessed December 2022)

Royal Society for the Protection of Birds, 'Breeding Birds, Nests, Eggs and Songs' (rspb.org.uk) (accessed December 2022)

Sneeboer, Sneeboer.com (accessed December 2022)

UK Centre for Ecology & Hydrology, 'Hedgerow Management and Rejuvenation' (ceh.ac.uk) (accessed December 2022)

The Wildlife Trusts, 'How to Manage a Hedgerow for Wildlife' (wildlifetrusts.org) (accessed December 2022)

Chapter 8 Composts and Growing Media

Einstein A., *'To Margot Einstein, After His Sister Maja's Death'* (1951)

Growing Solutions Incorporated, growingsolutions.com (accessed December 2022)

Horticulture Trades Association, *'Growing Media'* (hta.org.uk) (accessed December 2022)

The International Union for the Conservation of Nature, *'The State of UK Peatlands: an update'* (iucn.org 2019) (accessed December 2022)

The International Union for the Conservation of Nature Peatland Programme (iucn-uk-peatlandprogramme.org) (accessed December 2022)

Joint Nature Conservation Committee, *'Towards an Assessment of the State of UK Peatlands'* (jncc.gov.uk 2011) (accessed December 2022)

Permaculture Research Institute, *'Compost Teas and Extracts: Brewin' and Bubblin' Basics'* (permaculturenews.org 2012) (accessed December 2022)

Stern N., *'The Economics of Climate Change: The Stern Review'* (webarchive.nationalarchives.gov.uk 2010) (accessed December 2022)

Chapter 9 Productive Growing

Charles K., *'Food Production Emissions Make Up More Than a Third of Global Total'* (Newscientist.com 2021) (accessed December 2022)

Green Futures, Grimsby greenfuturesgrimsby.co.uk (accessed December 2022)

Mollison W., Permaculturenoosa.com.au, 2018 (accessed December 2022)

Chapter 10 Garden Maintenance

Floral Daily, floraldaily.com

Royal Horticultural Society, *'10 Ways to be More Sustainable in Your Garden'* (accessed December 2022)

Chapter 11 Water in the Garden

Royal Horticultural Society, *'Rain Gardens'* (rhs.org.uk) (accessed December 2022)

Chapter 12 Habitat Creation

Freshwater Habitats Trust, freshwaterhabitats.org.uk, (accessed December 2022)

Hardy, E. and Stewart D., *'Butterfly City'* (pattfoundation.org 2019) (accessed December 2022)

Joint Nature Conservation Committee, *'UK Biodiversity Action Plan (UK BAP)'* (jncc.gov.uk 2019) (accessed December 2022)

Piper R., *'Saproxylic Beetles'* (rosspiper.net 2020) (accessed December 2022)

Royal Society, *'What is the State of Biodiversity in the UK?'* (royalsociety.org) (accessed December 2022)

Royal Horticultural Society, *'Wildlife Ponds'* (rhs.org.uk) (accessed December 2022)

Royal Society for the Protection of Birds, *'Breeding Birds, Nests, Eggs and Songs'* (rspb.org.uk) (accessed December 2022)

William, P., Biggs, J., Nicolet, P., *New Clean-Water Ponds — a New Way to Protect Freshwater Biodiversity* (British Wildlife, 2010)

Wilson E. O., E O Wilson Biodiversity Foundation 2018

FURTHER RESOURCES

Big Butterfly Count
  bigbutterflycount.butterfly-conservation.org
Big Garden Birdwatch
  rspb.org.uk
Biodynamics Association
  biodynamics.com
Botanical society of Britain and Ireland
  bsbi.org
Buglife
  buglife.org.uk
Butterfly Conservation
  butterfly-conservation.org
Centre for Ecology and Hydrology
  ceh.ac.uk
Dr Ross Piper
  rosspiper.net/2020/01/10/saproxylic-beetles/
Ethical Trading Initiative
  ethicaltrade.org
Fairtrade stone
  marshalls.co.uk
Freshwater Habitats Trust
  freshwaterhabitats.org.uk
Growing solutions
  growingsolutions.com
Heronswood Garden
  heronswoodgarden.org
International Union for the Conservation of Nature (IUCN)
  iucn-uk-peatlandprogramme.org
Joint Nature Conservancy Committee
  jncc.gov.uk
Living wage
  livingwage.org.uk

Permaculture Association
  permaculture.org.uk
Peter Korn
  peterkornstradgard.se
Phyto Studio
  phytostudio.com
Plantlife
  plantlife.org.uk
Royal Horticultural Society
  rhs.org.uk
Royal Society for the Protection of Birds
  rspb.org.uk
Seedy Sunday
  seedysunday.org
Soil Association
  soilassociation.org
Square Foot Gardening
  squarefootgardening.org
St Andrews Botanical Gardens
  standrewsbotanic.org
Sustainable Soils Alliance
  sustainablesoils.org
The Wildlife Trusts
  wildlifetrusts.org
Trees and Design Action Group
  tdag.org.uk
Treezilla
  treezilla.org
Trussell Trust
  www.trusselltrust.org

ACKNOWLEDGEMENTS

When tasked to write a book within a new and developing field of study, one requires two fundamentals: agility of thought and a reliable compass to guide your path. Sustainable gardening, as a new field of study, is rapidly evolving and developing. Concepts are constantly being developed, challenged and refined. The author must, therefore, be capable of agile thought, critical analysis and the ability to amend and develop arguments as our knowledge of this fascinating area of study grows. This process carries a risk that the author deviates from their path, and ends up wandering aimlessly through the topic, like a tourist in a new land that is yet to be discovered. A reliable compass is, therefore, a vital tool.

If this book is to be successful in informing, guiding and encouraging the reader through the myriad decisions faced when trying to create or manage a garden or designed landscape, this is due in no small way to an incredible team of visionary people who coached the author in agile thinking, and who were his reliable compass. A huge debt of thanks is due to Sheri-Leigh Miles, who introduced me to sustainability some years ago, and who so ably critiqued and helped to develop the early draft. Claudia West of Phyto Studio and Dr Sally O'Halloran, Associate Professor at the Norwegian University of Life Sciences, shared their approaches to the design and creation of sustainable, ecologically functioning landscapes. The Swedish plantsman and designer Peter Korn introduced new perspectives in plant selection and management.

Caroline Jackson and Glynis Maynard, who are Professional Associates at the Royal Horticultural Society (and long-suffering colleagues) patiently explained, challenged, critiqued and offered new perspectives. Janet Manning, one of the leading horticultural water-management consultants in the UK, has relentlessly challenged, nurtured and developed both my thinking and understanding on countless issues. Rebecca Slack, the coordinator of Plant Network, provided the opportunity to share and test developing theories and models of thinking by kindly inviting contributions at their conferences and sustainability workshops. These opportunities allowed a wider audience to critique the concepts discussed.

Finally, a huge thank you is due to Dr Sue Moss, Head of Education and Learning at the Royal Horticultural Society, for her untiring support, her sound advice and for agreeing to write the foreword to this book.

This book is genuinely a team effort.

The errors are mine.

The brilliance is theirs.

Thank you.

It simply would not have been possible without you.

INDEX